INCENTIVES FOR RESEARCH, DEVELOPMENT, AND INNOVATION IN PHARMACEUTICALS

T0224276

SERIES ECONOMÍA DE LA SALUD Y GESTIÓN SANITARIA
Edited by **Vicente Ortún**

Title on the series

INCENTIVES FOR RESEARCH, DEVELOPMENT, AND INNOVATION IN PHARMACEUTICALS

WALTER GARCÍA-FONTES (DIR.)
Departamento de Economía y Empresa
Universidad Pompeu Fabra, Barcelona

Springer Healthcare

Series *Economía de la salud y gestión sanitaria*
Edited by *Vicente Ortún, CRES-UPF*

Springer Healthcare

Springer Healthcare Ibérica SL.
Calle Arte 27- 2° A - 28033
Madrid | Spain
www.springerhealthcare.com

Although every effort has been made to ensure that drug doses and other information are presented accurately in this publication, the ultimate responsibility rests with the prescribing physician. Neither the publisher nor the authors can be held responsible for errors or for any consequences arising from the use of the information contained herein. Any product mentioned in this publication should be used in accordance with the prescribing information prepared by the manufacturers. No claims or endorsements are made for any drug or compound at present under clinical investigation.

ISBN 978-84-938062-1-7
DOI 10.1007/978-84-938062-7-9
Depósito Legal: M-47.442-2011

ISBN 978-84-938062-7-9 (eBook)

Table of contents

Authors

JOAN-RAMÓN BORRELL

Joan-Ramon Borrell is Associate Professor in Economics at the University of Barcelona, Spain. He is member of the Governments and Markets Research Group. He is Research Fellow at the Public-Private Sector Research Center at IESE Business School (University of Navarra), and at the Health Economics Research Center (CRES) at the University Pompeu Fabra. His main research is at the cross-roads of industrial and public economics. He models empirically the strategic interaction of firms in markets, such as the market for pharmaceuticals or for energy. Using the estimates of models, he identifies and quantifies the impact of public policies on firm conduct, as well as the adequacy of such policies to achieve government targets, and also the overall effect of public policies on welfare.

WALTER GARCÍA-FONTES

Walter Garcia-Fontes is an associate professor at the Department of Economics and Business of Universitat Pompeu Fabra. His research interests are in Industrial Organization, firm innovation, technological change and applied econometrics. He has published his work in leading international field journals. He has coordinated various projects in the European Commission Framework Programmes studying the European chemical industry and the organizational changes related to new industrial relations.

LOUIS GARRISON

Lou Garrison is Professor and Associate Director in the Pharmaceutical Outcomes Research and Policy Program, Department of Pharmacy, at the University of Washington in Seattle. His recent research focuses on designing and conducting economic and outcomes research evaluations of pharmaceutical, biotechnology, and diagnostic products, and on policy issues related to pricing and reimbursement, regulatory risk-benefit analysis, and pharmacogenetics.

HENRY GRABOWSKI

Henry G. Grabowski has been at Duke University since 1972 where he is Professor Emeritus of Economics and Director of the Program in Pharmaceuticals and Health Economics. He received his Ph.D. in economics from Princeton University in 1967. He has held visiting appointments at the Health Care Financing Administration in Washington, D.C., and the International Institute of Management in Berlin, Germany. Professor Grabowski has published numerous studies on the pharmaceutical industry, with his principal research involving the economics of the innovation process, government regulation, and market competition. He has been an advisor to the National Academy of Sciences, the Institute of Medicine, the Federal Trade Commission, and the Congressional Budget Office. He has testified before Congress several times on policy issues involving pharmaceuticals and the health care sector.

AIDAN HOLLIS

Aidan Hollis is Professor in Economics at the University of Calgary, and Vice-President of Incentives for Global Health, a US-based NGO focused on the development of the Health Impact Fund proposal. Hollis studied at Cambridge University and the University of Toronto, where he obtained a PhD in economics. His research focuses on innovation and competition in pharmaceutical markets, though he has published over thirty peer reviewed articles and two books in a range of fields of economics. In 2003-4 he served as the T.D. MacDonald Chair in Industrial Economics at the Competition Bureau. He has provided expert reports and testimony in a variety of pharmaceutical-related cases in Federal, Appeals and Supreme Court cases in Canada, and has advised companies and governments.
For more information, see the websites: http://econ.ucalgary.ca/hollis.htm and http://healthimpactfund.org

MARY MORAN

Dr Moran is Director of Policy Cures, an independent research group based in Sydney and London. She has over 20 years experience in health policy and practice, including 10 years specialising in policy related to neglected disease R&D. Mary is an Honorary Senior Lecturer at the London School of Hygiene and Tropical Medicine, and an Expert Adviser to the World Health Organisation, European Commission, European and Developing Countries Clinical Trials Partnership, Global Alliance for Vaccines and Immunisation (GAVI),

OECD and the Wellcome Trust. She was previously a doctor, diplomat, and policy analyst with Medecins Sans Frontieres.

RUHT PUIG-PEIRÓ

Ruth's current research focus is on economic appraisal methods across UK government departments, relative effectiveness and health technology assessment across European countries, and the economics of the pharmaceutical industry. Before joining the OHE in 2010, Ruth held positions as a Research Officer at the Personal Social Services Research Unit (PSSRU) at the London School of Economics and Political Science and a Researcher at the Centre for Research in Economics and Health (CRES) at Universitat Pompeu Fabra in Barcelona, Spain.

ADRIAN TOWSE

Adrian Towse is Visiting Professor at the University of York and a Visiting Senior Researcher at the Department of Public Health and Primary Care at the University of Oxford. For ten years, he served as the Non-Executive Director of the Oxford Radcliffe Hospitals NHS Trust, one of the UK's largest hospitals. Adrian joined the OHE in 1993. Adrian Towse has been Director of the Office of Heath Economics since 1992.

His interests include the use of "risk-sharing" arrangements between health care payers and pharmaceutical companies to manage the introduction of new health technologies; the economics of pharmacogenetics for health care payers and for the pharmaceutical industry; economic issues around the use of public private partnerships for the development of treatments for less developed country diseases; and the economics of medical negligence - incentive properties and costs of 'no fault' versus reformed tort procedures.

CHAPTER 1

Introduction

Walter García-Fontes

This book deals with incentives to innovation, with a special focus on the pharmaceutical sector. A relevant issue in most industries, as innovation has been regarded as an engine for economic growth that most governments want to promote, it is particularly relevant in the pharmaceutical industry, where not all social needs provide equally profitable opportunities and where most OECD countries strive to implement different measures to promote research in these less profitable areas. This issue becomes particularly dramatic when we take into account diseases mostly affecting low income countries and diseases affecting small groups of patients, where research into vaccines and new drugs is limited or non existent.

How can incentives be provided to deal with these less profitable activities when no clear markets exist for the innovations being introduced? This is one of the key issues in providing incentives in these less profitable areas, as it is well known that it is very hard to find an adequate substitute for the private incentives provided by actual markets. Public intervention is no fit substitute for a market and very often results in suboptimal allocation of resources. Some of the contributions of this book discuss alternative mechanisms to substitute for inexistent markets, as traditional mechanisms such as public procurement or direct subsidies have proven totally insufficient. There has also been a clear mismatch between the size of the markets being targeted and the incentives being provided. Some of the contributions of this book go in the direction of first accurately identifying the size of each disease market, as well as the characteristics of the products and the developers, before considering setting up any type of incentive scheme, and what could be called a new matching mechanism between products and developers.

The problem is made more acute by the fact that the other main traditional mechanisms to provide incentives for innovation, i.e. the protection of intellectual property rights, also fails in the absence of markets. The patent system is the main instrument that has been used to give private players sufficient incentives to invest in new products and processes that may have a high social value and therefore may provide returns beyond the profits that the innovator firm may appropriate. But the patent system works if it provides additional profits within a well defined market. And even with strong markets the patent system has been regarded as not always providing the right incentives for innovation, which is why other channels have been proposed, such as market size as an indication of future profit opportunities, information instruments to reduce demand uncertainty, and other instruments such as trade secrets.

Patents become ineffective in incentivizing R&D when appropriability is low, that is, when firms are unable to obtain a sufficient return on their products to cover for the risky investments involved. This stems not only from the traditional problem of social value being larger than private value, but also from the minute size of the markets in many of the areas where R&D would be badly needed for product development. Are there any alternatives? Some ideas are provided in this book. For instance, granting a period of data exclusivity to firms that develop new drugs, during which no generic firm can enter on the basis of clinical trial data presented to regulatory authorities in order to be approved. Other mechanisms rely to a greater extent on direct government funding or, increasingly, on private foundation funding to fill the gap when patents are not providing a sufficiently strong incentive.

The other key vehicle for R&D incentives in the pharmaceutical sector is directly related to the existing markets in developed countries. What is the flow of inventive activity in the developed world? What health plans are in place in the United States, the European Union and Japan, and what role do they play in the introduction of new products? This book provides a cross-cutting comparative analysis of the introduction of new pharmaceutical products to advance in the understanding of the role of the different regulatory systems and their influence in the flows of inventive activity internationally.

Other more controversial mechanisms to foster incentives in the pharmaceutical industry are being proposed. Generally speaking, pharmaceutical companies expect to obtain sufficient returns from their hefty R&D investments, but this is not always the case in all countries. If the performance of new products could be measured and make explicit both to users and suppliers, the returns that firms get would be closer to what they expect, and payers would be better inclined to accept having to pay —either directly or through subsidies— for the value they receive. This is the so called pay for performance mechanism for drugs. Despite its apparent conceptual simplicity, it has proved highly controversial for most of the players involved. There are vast problems relating to information —as in any regulation of private information—,transaction costs and implementation of the mechanism. Still, the benefits are clear: incentives for otherwise hard to finance new products, improved efficiency of the industry through better rewarding investments, and reduced uncertainties overall. What is the net result? This book provides evidence that may make this type of mechanism more attractive to the industry.

It follows from the above that pricing schemes, both upstream and downstream in the industry, should be studied more carefully to understand their influence on R&D investment decisions and projects pursued in the industry.

The authors featured in this book have provided different insights on the issues involved in R&D incentives in the pharmaceutical industry, all of them clearly and simply explained and providing policy recommendations whenever possible, in the hope that the different analyses contained here may prove useful both for industry practitioners, health regulators and policy makers, and academic researchers.

Executive summary

Chapter 2 - Incentives for innovation: a survey

The second chapter, by Walter García-Fontes, provides a general survey on the economic literature on the incentives for innovation. This is a central issue in innovation theory, since its understanding is crucial for the formulation of technological policy. Private agents fund innovation privately if they have enough prospects of a reasonable return for their investments, while other agents, such as academic researchers or public-private consortia, may receive incentives in the form of an enhanced personal reputation or career advancements. The survey reviews the most significant theories and empirical research results on the different factors and determinants affecting incentives for innovation.

Chapter 3 - Incentives for innovation: neglected diseases

When the difference between social benefit and private benefit is very large, there may be no private incentives at all to innovate. This is the case of so-called "neglected diseases", which are analyzed by Mary Moran in chapter 3. Are there markets for drugs for this type of diseases? Can heavily publicly-subsidized drugs obtained through subsidized research operate in common markets? What are the mechanisms to provide incentives for innovation when no traditional markets can operate for these drugs? Moran proposes a number of instruments and schemes to improve the prospects of incentives for innovation for drugs aimed at neglected diseases.

Chapter 4 - When patents are not enough: supplementary incentives for pharmaceutical innovation

Aidan Hollis provides in chapter 4 an analysis of the limits of the patent system in the pharmaceutical industry. As with the drugs analyzed in the preceding chapter, there are situations where the value of the patent reward is low compared to the social value of the innovations. In these cases firms will underinvest in innovation despite the high social value of the potential invention. Hollis proposes mechanisms alternative to patents, such as the Health Impact Fund, which may be useful for neglected diseases, and may also be used more broadly in the pharmaceutical industry.

Chapter 5 - The contribution of the United States, Europe and Japan in discovering new drugs: 1982-2003

Chapter 5, by Henry Grabovsky, analyzes the different instruments that have been put in place in the United States to improve the position of this country in the worldwide pharmaceutical industry. There has been public support for basic biomedical research and for the transfer of basic research from universities, and further support has come from private and public equity markets. As regards demand, the growth of managed care plans and pharmacy benefit management firms has improved the prospects of drug benefits. The overall result has been that the United States is now the world leader in the discovery and introduction of innovative new drug groups such as first-in-class, biotech, global, and orphan products. This chapter provides a fine example of how public policy on biopharmaceutical innovation may provide the right incentives for innovation. The instruments, which interact with each other, include support for basic research and technology transfers, intellectual property protection, regulation of product safety and efficacy, and pricing schemes.

Chapter 6 - The use of pay-for-performance for drugs. Can it improve incentives for innovation?

In the sixth chapter of this book, Adrian Towse, Lou Garrison and Ruth Puig-Peiro present an analysis of the consequences of performance-based pay for drugs and its effect on incentives for innovation. As set out in chapter 3, price regulation may discourage R&D investment as it may preclude reasonable returns if not implemented correctly. Paying for performance may constitute a transparent mechanism where buyers know how much they are paying and companies have the right incentive to pursue future innovations. Nevertheless, health care providers are reluctant to adopt this type of price mechanisms and further research may be needed to grasp all the implications. The chapter provides a discussion that helps to understand these pricing schemes, with examples that show their advantages and disadvantages and analyze their value as an incentive for innovation.

Chapter 7 - Drug Price Regulation: Recent Trends and Downstream Neglected Issues

In chapter 7, Joan Ramón Borrell surveys the literature on price regulation in the pharmaceutical sector. Price regulation has been used as a mechanism for the provision of approved drugs, which in turn assures pharmaceutical firms a stream of revenues for their future growth. The most traditional pricing schemes, anchored in cost-based regulation/procurement schemes, have increasingly been transformed into two-tiered price controls in most developed countries. These follow two strategies. For in-patent drugs, incentive regulation and procurement are based on revenue-sharing agreements, incentives to providers and demand management. For out-of-patent and generic drugs, on the other hand, the main mechanisms in place have been price regulation/procurement. The key issue is what is the role of wholesalers and pharmacists, and whether pricing is sufficiently efficient to assure a healthy stream of upstream innovation.

CHAPTER 2

Incentives to innovate: a survey

Walter García-Fontes

Introduction

Incentives to innovate are a central element of innovation theory and the understanding of how incentives work is crucial for the formulation of a sensible technological policy. From a private point of view, innovators privately fund innovation and then use intellectual property protection mechanisms to appropriate returns from these investments. For other types of agents, such as academic researchers or public-private consortia, the incentives may also involve personal reputation and career advancements.

What are the corporate incentives to engage in basic research or applied research? Do academic researchers find incentives to devote time to applied research? These questions are relevant in the current debate on the effects of the strength of intellectual property rights. The adoption of the Bayh-Dole Act in the US, for instance, presumed that firms had no incentives to invest in downstream R&D aimed at developing university inventions, since the outcome of this research may go to the public domain. The empirical evidence on patenting and licensing does not provide strong support to this argument. In several technological areas, such as biomedical technologies for example, patents protect different types of knowledge, ranging from product technologies —which are almost directly marketable— to process technologies with a more basic content. The research process itself, and the institutional setting within which that research is conducted, with different types of contracts when collaboration is involved, may affect the characteristics of the outcome, i.e. the patent intended to protect this research.

Therefore, there is a need to balance incentives in all organizations engaged in R&D. Different organizations have different goals and do not attach the same value to scientific results and commercial prospects. In the pharmaceutical industry, investments in basic research may not produce immediate profits but are crucial for long-term capabilities and for the ability of firms to continuously innovate their products. On the other hand, academic institutions and basic research centers are depending increasingly on the revenues produced by patents, licenses and contract research, as government funding has been decreasing. So there is a need for a balance of incentives in increasing knowledge in general and in obtaining revenue-producing patents and licenses.

In this survey we provide an overview of the different examples in the literature that have tried to analyze the issue of incentives in the collaboration between agents with different goals, objectives and interests, such as universities, public laboratories and firms.

Incentives to innovate

Incentives for innovation may come through different channels. On the one hand, strategic interaction of firms in the marketplace may affect the prospects that firms have in investing in R&D or any other activities that may increase the possibilities to innovate. On the other hand, the pressure of a higher market demand or a reduction in demand uncertainty may also give firms more incentives to increase their innovation rate. Foreign direct investments may also have an effect on how domestic firms view innovative activities and how much they invest in them. And finally there are also contractual problems that may mitigate the conflict of interests between the agents involved in innovation activities.

Competition and innovation

The seminal contribution to the analysis of the incentives to innovate is Arrow (1962). In a simple model of cost-reducing innovation he compares the incentives in terms of profit of different market structures, and his main result shows that firms in competitive environments have a larger incentive to innovate than firms that sustain market power. The simple intuition behind the result is that a competitive firm has much more to gain than a monopolistic firm, as the latter already has profits above competitive levels without innovating.

The empirical literature on the relation between innovation and competition has faced the problem of the direction of causality. The early literature has used market structure as an explanatory variable, but the causality might run in the opposite direction. Innovation may affect market structure for different reasons. For instance, it is reasonable to assume that R&D involves fixed costs, or that innovation will change the pattern of firm growth in different sectors changing their market structure, or finally it will change the efficient scale of production, thereby affecting the number and size of firms.

A number of studies have addressed these issues empirically. Blundell et al. (1999), for instance, find a robust and positive effect of market share on innovation using a sample of British manufacturing firms. Aghion et al. (2005) on their part, find evidence that the relation between competition and innovation shows an inverted U shape, indicating that it is a non-monotonic relationship. Finally, Tang (2006), using a sample of Canadian manufacturing firms, obtains that incentives to innovate depend on the measure of competition used. His main conclusion is that the relationship between competition and innovation is ambiguous, as it depends on specific competition perception and specific innovation activity.

More recently, and given the non-conclusive results of field data research on the relationship between competition and incentives for innovation, there have been attempts to study this issue in the laboratory through experiments. An example of this literature is Darai et al. (2010). They analyze the effects of competition on R&D investments aimed at process innovations. By increasing the number of firms or switching from Cournot to Bertrand competition, they attempt to assess the effects on R&D investments. They use an experiment that mimics a two-stage game where in the first stage firms decide the level of R&D investments, and in the second stage they compete in the product market. They find that an increase in the number of firms reduces R&D investments, but a switch from Cournot to Bertrand competition increases investments.

Demand as an incentive to innovation

The consideration of demand characteristics as an incentive to innovation is an old topic in the literature on innovation. For instance, Schmookler (1962) proposed that the size of the market and the prospects of firm markups shape the rate and direction of innovations. This has been called the incentive effect of demand on innovation, according to which market demand has a multiplier effect on innovation through firm markups. Thus, market demand is viewed as a source of economic incentives for invention. Expected demand, proxied by the size of the market, is important to assess future profits, and therefore the incentives to innovate should be positively correlated with the size of the market or any other variable that provides information about future profitability.

Another strong effect of market demand on innovation is what has been called the uncertainty effect, which refers to the channeling to firms of knowledge about market needs. This reduces uncertainty about future firm profits and therefore stimulates innovation.

The direct demand effect may have stronger effects on process innovations, as it is easier to forecast their effect, while the uncertainty effect may impact on product innovations. Fontana and Guerzoni (2008) have used a sample of small and medium sized European firms to empirically analyze these two effects. Using market size as a proxy for future demand, they find that economic incentives of this kind have a positive impact on the innovation rate, especially for process innovations. On the other hand using contacts with costumers as a measure of the reduction of uncertainty, they also find that firms that use this channel more often consider product innovation as their most important innovation.

Incentives provided by foreign direct investments

Foreign direct investments have been found to have effects on the performance of domestic firms in host countries. Technological synergies between foreign firms and domestic firms may provide additional incentives for innovation, and this has been used by policymakers to try to stimulate the competitiveness of local industries, the most prominent example being China, where aggressive policies were put into place to attract foreign direct investment inflows and to try to create synergies with local firms.

The channel through which foreign direct investments may affect innovation incentives is not clear. The entry of multinational firms may lead to an increase in competition and provide an incentive to local firms to increase their efficiency or to search for innovations to maintain their competitiveness. The main channel through which these positive effects may arise are the so-called demonstration externalities. The idea is that domestic firms can improve their efficiency, organization or products, by formal and informal contacts with foreign firms, that is, by observing their productive processes, exchanging workers, or transacting with foreign suppliers or clients. But the effect of more foreign competition can also be negative, if domestic firms are not able to compete and find themselves lagging technologically, or if they have to face new restrictions to the access of production factors.

Brambilla et al. (2009) propose an additional channel and emphasize innovation and imitation incentives for domestic firms, which face increased competition from foreign firms. They propose a partial-equilibrium model with firms of different productivity levels, where domestic firms may either innovate by introducing a new product line or imitate an existing product line. Testing the predictions of their model with a sample of Chinese manufacturing firms, they find that the main incentives for local firms come through the imitation channel, especially for medium sized firms with originally low exposure to international competition.

Incentives and contracts

Chen and Sappington (2011) extend Aghion and Bolton's (1987) model of exclusive contracts to analyze the case where R&D is relevant. In many industries where innovation and R&D drive firm performance, contracts that promote exclusivity may arise. Chen and Sappington show that the effects of exclusive contracts depend on the patent protection level and the relative R&D abilities of participating firms. They find that an exclusive contract that reduces R&D for an entrant can increase welfare when there is excessive R&D due to strong patent protection. In contrast, an exclusive contract can reduce welfare when R&D ability is high.

Knowledge from universities is transferred to the private sector mainly by licensing agreements, which is the most commonly used method, or by the creation of spin-offs.

The transfer of publicly funded knowledge to downstream firms has been the subject of extensive research. Cockburn and Henderson (1998) examine this transfer in the pharmaceutical industry, where there is extensive public support for research and the industry is science-intensive. As Cohen and Levinthal (1989) argued in a seminal paper, the upstream scientific base spurs innovation in the pharmaceutical industry but through large investments in complementary in-house basic research and important changes in internal organization. These are costly investments in what these authors have called "absorptive capacity", that is, the investments necessary to accumulate knowledge and skills and to manage the organization in such a way that external knowledge may be used. Cockburn and Henderson argue that it is also important for pharmaceutical firms to establish direct connections with the scientific community to be able to incorporate upstream scientific results into their product innovation.

Another interesting issue is the balance of incentives between time dedicated to basic research and time dedicated to commercial development. This is especially relevant, given that in several countries, for instance in the US with the Bayh-Dole Act, incentives are put into place so that researchers usually rewarded for basic research devote more time to the commercial development of their knowledge and to generate revenues through patents or licenses.

Banal-Estañol and Macho-Stadler (2010) propose a model to analyze these incentives. In a repeated model a researcher has to decide how much time is to be devoted to produce new innovative ideas which have both scientific and commercial value, or use prior research and develop it into a commercially valid innovation. In their results they show that the introduction of commercial objectives for the researchers not only increases the time dedicated to commercial development, but also affects the basic research program, inducing them to undertake riskier programs that could produce high-quality ideas. They also characterize the optimal incentive scheme showing how to induce research-oriented firms into an optimal balance of incentives, and showing that even for non-scientific-oriented firms it may be optimal to recruit scientists to provide the right incentives for conducting research.

Patents and the incentives to innovate

We now turn to patents, the main instrument currently being used by technological policy to provide incentives for firms to innovate. The existence of patents has been justified by the public good nature of innovation and as a means to appropriate the returns of R&D investments.

Patents: length, scope and breadth

The main argument in favor of patents as an incentive to innovate is that they encourage *ex ante* innovation by creating *ex post* monopoly rents.

Arrow (1962) argues in a seminal work that firms will underinvest in R&D from a social welfare point of view because they cannot fully appropriate the benefits of their investments in R&D. Intellectual property rights can be a way of dealing with this problem. Arrow also discusses several types of contracts that can be superior to patents in certain situations. Another seminal contribution on patents is the theoretical study made by Nordhaus (1969), who analyzes the social and private costs and benefits of the patent system and establishes the optimal length of the patent from society's point of view. He presents the social impact of the patent system as a trade-off between the dynamic efficiency created by stronger incentives to innovate and the monopolistic inefficiencies that a longer protection period introduces.

Beyond the optimal length of a patent, more recent work has focused on the optimal breadth or scope, or combinations of these different dimensions. The scope of a patent is more difficult to measure than its length, and different approaches have been proposed in the literature. Gilbert and Shapiro (1990) have proposed looking at the ability of the holder of the patent to raise its price, while Klemperer (1990) has looked at the impact on close substitutes, and Lerner (1994) has focused on the number of side classifications.

More recently, Acemoglu et al. (2011) propose an alternative rationale for the existence of patents. They present a model where patents help potential innovators to experiment with the new knowledge and allow a more efficient *ex post* transfer, which is socially beneficial.

The rationale for the existence of patents as an incentive to innovate also comes from the literature on patent races. Here the idea is that when several firms race for an innovation, they may arrive to a successful outcome independently, and so some legal rule has to be put into place to determine who owns the innovation. A weak form of protection is trade secret protection, where all innovators are allowed to use the innovation, while a stronger form is patent protection, where only the first inventors get an exclusive right, or following the expression used in this literature, the winner takes all.

From an empirical point of view, there has been extensive literature seeking to assess the impact of the patent system on social welfare. Among others, Mansfield (1981) and Scherer (1980) have suggested that there is a considerable difference between the high social return and the private return to innovation. They find that behind the difference between social and private returns there is the rate of imitation, which causes underinvestment in private R&D, and which may justify the existence of the patent system. In any case, imitation is costly and time-consuming, suggesting that there are a lot of other factors besides patents that may hinder or favor imitation, and that it is not clear what would happen if the patent system was changed.

In a very well known empirical study, Manfield (1986) analyzed the effects of the patent system on the rate of innovation with a sample of US firms. He finds that the patent system has a small effect on most industries with the exception of pharmaceuticals and chemicals where the patent system is essential to protect the large investments needed to incorporate the upstream knowledge base into product innovation. Nevertheless, Mansfield remarks that most industries make extensive use of the patent system creating a so-called "patenting paradox". From 1960 to 1980 there was much talk on the declining productivity in R&D although there was no decline in the propensity to patent in most industries (on this issue, see the work of Grilliches, 1980; 1989 and 1990; and Hall, 1994).

Other studies have conducted surveys to collect direct data on the effects of patents and how they influence the incentive o innovate. The one known as the "Yale study" interviewed hundreds of R&D managers on the role of patents in different industrial sectors (Levin, 1986; Levin et al., 1987; Klevorick et al., 1995). They found that there are important variations between the different sectors in appropriability conditions and in the role of patents. In general, the empirical literature has found that the appropriability of R&D investments depends heavily on elements other than patents, such as secrecy and lead times.

Patents as incentives to innovation in developing countries

Do patent laws provide incentives to entrepreneurs in developing countries to make risky investments in technology innovation? Do patent laws facilitate the development of technology markets among public-private technology innovation networks? Do patent laws facilitate North-South technology innovation collaborations?

Incentives for innovation in developing countries have long been a concern for the diffusion of innovations. Since the 1994 World Trade Organization Agreement, all WTO member countries are required to meet certain minimum standards of intellectual property law and enforcement. The consequence has been that developing countries started to provide higher levels of protection. There has been substantial research devoted to understanding whether indigenous technology innovation should be promoted in developing countries.

This debate has generated considerable theoretical and empirical literature during the last decades. For instance, Helpman (1993) has proposed a two-region general equilibrium model where he considers alternatively exogenous and endogenous rates of innovation. Considering imitation only as the technological activity of the less developed regions, Helpman shows that, in the absence of foreign investment, tightening intellectual property rights does not entail additional benefits for the developing country. He shows that even when the rate of innovation is responsive to IPR, there is an initial rise in the rate of innovation but it is only temporary and it is offset by subsequent declines.

Two other examples of theoretical discussions of the same issue are Lai and Qiu (2001) and Grossman and Lai (2002). They analyze both innovation and imitation and measure the level of protection by analyzing the optimal length of the patents in two situations: before and after the change in the WTO international agreements. One of their main results shows that the greater the protection in the developed country, the lower the optimal patent length in the developing country.

Following these theoretical debates, there have been several empirical studies that have addressed this issue.

For instance, McCalman (2001) estimates the increase in the value of patents granted to foreigners and of patents outstanding abroad for a sample of developing and developed countries. According to his calculations all of the developing and some developed countries in his sample end up in a worse situation after the application of the WTO agreements.

Forero-Pineda (2006) finds that the possible positive effect of stronger IPR protection in developing countries could be more than negatively offset by the negative impact on the domestic scientific community, since international scientific exchanges may be hindered, and positive externalities to local scientific communities may not happen.

Another example is Ryan (2010), who presents a study of five post-patent law reforms in bio-medical technology invention and innovation projects in the state of Sao Paulo, in Brazil. His results support the proposition that patents have provided more incentives to Brazilian bio-medical technology entrepreneurs to make risky investments into innovation. He also finds that the increased patentability has facilitated technology markets among public-private technology innovation networks.

Quality of patents

A final and important topic is that not all patents are equally valuable and there is a considerable skewness in the distribution of any variable related to the quality of patents. Different measures have been used to assess the value of a patent.

Meyer and Tang (2007) offer a survey of the different methods that have been proposed to assess the quality of patents. The list of indicators of quality as well as its determinants is quite extensive. In both sets of information (but not simultaneously) it is possible to find characteristics of the patents, including the number of citations, family size, number of claims, technological scope, and whether the patent was ever opposed or litigated.

Sapsalis and Van Pottelsberghe de la Potterie (2007) propose additional determinants of patent value based on institutional sources of knowledge used to produce the patent and on the geographic scope of patenting strategy. They apply these new indicators of patent value to a sample of academic patents from Belgian universities. They find that after controlling for the age and the technological field the most important value determinant of an academic patent is its number of backward patent citations. They also find that self-backward patent citations show a lower patent value, probably reflecting an invention of a more incremental nature. With respect to geographical scope, they find that expanding the patent to the USA or Japan increases the value of the patent.

The open source software model of innovation

A model of innovation where almost no pecuniary or monetary incentives exist for innovators it the so-called open innovation model. One example of this model is the open source model of innovation. There has been some recent research into the incentives behind this type of model of innovation, as their understanding may help in explaining incentives for innovation in general.

The most radical model of sharing is the so-called "private-collective innovation model", according to the term coined by Hippel and von Krogh (2003). In this model the innovator forgoes all instruments for the appropriation of returns generated by the innovation and only retains partial ownership of the intellectual property rights created. If there is no return from the innovation, where do the incentives in this type of innovations come from? At least where open source software is concerned, the incentives come from the rewards that the innovators get from the community. If they innovate and create a reputation of consistent behavior, i.e. they adhere the community's social standards, they can receive assistance and support for their developing tasks, they can improve their employment profile and they can increase their public reputation as a developer, which may in turn provide monetary rewards in the future. Some studies, such as Hertel et al. (2003) and Roberts et al. (2006) have shown that the rewards that the open source innovators obtain offset their contribution costs, therefore justifying their behavior from an economic point of view. There is in any case the question of why these open source projects are started before a community of developers comes into being that allows these mechanisms to start working. Gächter et al (2010) provide a theoretical model where they show that in a coordination game with multiple equilibria, a private-collective innovation configuration may be started up, and they support this model with experimental evidence about this behavior. Their empirical evidence shows that knowledge sharing in private-collective innovation involves social preferences in addition to material incentives. Thus, this innovation model may be influenced by fairness.

Concluding remarks

In recent decades there has been a substantial volume of economic and management literature devoted to understanding incentives for innovation and the role of patents and other intellectual property rights.

From a theoretical point of view, a rationale has been proposed for patents and other means of assuring some ex-post monopoly power to innovators. But there is also support for other channels stimulating innovation, such as the pressure of demand and market size, uncertainty reduction, or even reputation issues, as in the open innovation model.

From an empirical point of view there is still ample space for further research, as richer data sets and controlled natural or laboratory experiments are needed to provide more evidence on the direction of causality of innovation and its different incentives, as well as quantification of the effects involved.

REFERENCES

Acemoglu D, Bimpikis K, Ozdaglar A. Experimentation, patents and innovation. AEJ: Microeconomics. 2011;3:37-77.

Aghion P, Bolton P. Contracts as a Barrier to Entry. American Economic Review. 1987;77(3):388-401.

Aghion P, Bloom N, Blundel R, Griffith R, Howitt P. Competition and Innovation: an Inverted-U Relationship. Quarterly Journal of Economics. 2005;120:701-28.

Arrow K. Economic Welfare and the Allocation of Resources for Inventions. In: Nelson R, editor. The Rate and Direction of Inventive Activity. Princeton, NJ: Princeton University Press; 1962.

Basberg B. Patents and the measurement of technological change: A survey of the literature. Research Policy. 1987;16:131-141.

Brambilla I, Hale G, Long C. Foreign direct investment and the incentives to innovate and imitate. Scandinavian Journal of Economics. 2009;111(4):835-61.

Blundell R, Griffith R, Van Reenen J. Market Share, Market Value and Innovation in a Panel of British Manufacturing Firms. Review of Economic Studies. 1999;66:529-54.

Chen Y, Sappington DEM. Exclusive contracts, innovation and welfare. AEJ: Microeconomics. 2011;3:194-220.

Cockburn I, Henderson RM. Absorptive Capacity, Coauthoring Behavior, and the Organization of Research in Drug Discovery. Journal of Industrial Economics. 1998;46(2):157-82.

Cohen WM, Levintahl DA. Innovation and learning: the two faces of R&D. Economic Journal. 1989;99:569-96.

Darai D, Sacco D, Schmutzler A. Competition and innovation: an experimental investigation. Experimental Economics. 2010;13:439-60.

Fontana R, Guerzoni M. Incentives and uncertainty: an empirical analysis of the impact of demand on innovation. Cambridge Journal of Economics. 2008;32:927-46.

Gächter S, von Kroghb G, Haefligerb S. Initiating private-collective innovation: The fragility of knowledge sharing. Research Policy. 2010;39:893-906.

Gilbert R, Shapiro C. Optimal patent length and breadth. RAND Journal of Economics. 1990;21(1): 106-12.

Griliches, Z. R&D, Patents, and Productivity. Chicago, IL: University of Chicago Press; 1984.

Griliches Z. Patents: recent trends and puzzles. Brookings Papers on Economic Activity: Microeconomics. 1989;1:291-330.

Griliches Z. Patent statistics as economic indicators: a survey. Journal of Economic Literature. 1990; 28(4):1661-707.

Grossman G, Lai E. International Protection of Intellectual Property. NBER Working Paper No. 8704. Cambridge, January 2002.

Hall BH. Industrial Research during the 1980s: Did the Rate of Return Fall?. Cambridge, MA: NBER; 1994.

Helpman E. Innovation, imitation, and intellectual property rights. Econometrica. 1993;61: 1247-80.

Hertel G, Niedner S, Herrmann S. Motivation of Software Developers in open source Projects: an Internet-based survey of contributors to the Linux Kernel. Research Policy. 2003;32:1159-77.

Klemperer P. How broad should the scope of patent protection be? RAND Journal of Economics. 1990;21(1):113-30.

Klevorick AK, Levin RC, Nelson RR, Winter SG. On the source and significance of interindustry differences in technological opportunities. Research Policy. 1995;24(2):185-205.

Lai E, Qiu L. The North's Intellectual Property Rights - Standard for the South? City University of Hong Kong. Working Paper, October 2001.

Levin RC. A new look at the patent system. American Economic Review. 1986;76(2):199-202.

Levin RC, Klevorick NRR, Winter SG. Appropriating the Returns from Industrial Research and Development. Brooklings Papers on Economic Activity. 1987;3:783-831

Meyer M, Tang P. Exploring the value of academic patents: IP management practices in UK universities and their implication for third-stream indicators. Scientometrics. 2007;2:415-40.

Roberts J, Hann I-H, Slaughter S. Understanding the motivations participation and performance of open source software developers: a longitudinal study of the Apache projects. Management Science. 2006;52:984-99.

Ryan M. Patent incentives, technology markets and public-private bio-medical innovation networks in Brazil. World Development. 2010;38(8):1082-93.

Sapsalis E, Van Pottelsberghe de la Potterie B. The institutional sources of knowledge and the value of academic patents. Economics of Innovation and New Technologies. 2007;16(2):139-57.

Tang J. Competition and Innovation Behaviour. Research Policy. 2006;35:68-82.

von Hippel E, von Krogh G. Free revealing and the private-collective model of innovation incentives. R&D Management. 2006;36:295-306.

CHAPTER 3

Incentives for innovation: neglected diseases

Mary Moran

Introduction

Incentives to stimulate greater industry pharmaceutical innovation are in place in most OECD countries. However, they are never more needed than for so-called "neglected diseases" (NDs). These are diseases such as malaria, tuberculosis and helminth infections that afflict hundreds of millions of poor patients in developing countries. We focus here on how to stimulate industry innovation for these diseases, and on the circumstances in which alternative routes of innovation will be needed.

The Commission on Macroeconomics and Health allocated diseases to three categories depending on their commercial market returns[i]:
— Type I diseases have substantial commercial markets and R&D activity tailored to these, e.g. diabetes, hypertension.
— Type II diseases have modest, semi-commercial markets and a correspondingly modest level of R&D, e.g. travellers and military malaria, European TB.
— Type III diseases have virtually no commercial market and very limited R&D, e.g. Chagas disease, Buruli ulcer.

"Neglected diseases" traditionally comprise Type II and Type III diseases

Before going further, we offer two points that may seem commonsense, but which often bedevil discussions over incentives for neglected disease R&D. First, only a market is a market. A market is automatic, driven by supply and demand operating through the nexus of price, consumer funded, and flexible. Public funds, even in the form of

---

[i] Commission on Macroeconomics and Health (2001). Macroeconomics and Health: Investing in Health for Economic Development. Available from: http://whqlibdoc.who.int/publications/2001/924154550x.pdf [Accessed November 2010].

procurement funds, may not be a market in the usual sense. They are often not automatic; they frequently delink supply from demand (as does health insurance), since the purchaser is different from the consumer; and they are often both insecure, due to changes in government or government policy, and rigid.

The second point relates to patents and innovation. Patents are essentially a proxy for profits: they stimulate innovation by rewarding the innovator with monopoly rights to the market for an invention. If there is no profitable market, a patent is essentially valueless and thus plays little or no part in stimulating R&D. This is evidenced both by the lack of R&D for neglected diseases and by the willingness of companies to make their intellectual property (IP) freely available for neglected disease development by others (for example, patent pools and compound screening). A recent National Bureau of Economic Research (NBER) analysis of high, middle and low-income countries confirmed that:

> *"The difference between R&D effort directed at global diseases and neglected diseases is driven mainly by the difference in income of those affected, rather than a difference in patent protection alone"*[ii].

We note, however, that IP issues do play a role for Type II diseases such as HIV, which have commercial markets in the West as well as non-commercial markets in the developing world. They also come into play for domestic firms in the BRIC countries (Brazil, Russia, India and China), which may perceive the local neglected disease market as valuable. Though this can be an advantage if innovation for domestic patients is the desired outcome, generally speaking the main determinant —and opportunity— for neglected disease R&D is the complex balance between potential profits and potential costs.

Types of markets

Commercial (profitable) markets

If a market exists, innovation will be conducted (in the presence of patent protection) without the need for incentives directed to firms for which that market is sufficient. In practice, some diseases classified as Type II NDs fall into this category due to overlap with commercial markets in the West. For instance, overlapping Western market forces lead to creation of antibiotics for pneumonia and anti-retroviral drugs for AIDS. The key issue for these diseases is access, since patients with a purchasing power below that of the market are excluded from accessing treatments.

Borderline markets

If a market is borderline commercial, the cost-profit balance can be favourably tipped by government policy and regulation, at which point it will operate as a self-sustaining market with innovation generated by the prospect of profits. Many Type II and some Type III neglected diseases have borderline markets. These markets fall into two categories:

[ii] NBER Working Paper series: Investments in pharmaceuticals before and after TRIPS.

— The same product is suitable for Western and developing country markets —that is, no additional R&D must be undertaken to develop a product for global use— but, even collectively, the total market is borderline too small to be commercially attractive to most (or any) firms. For example, the market for malaria treatments, used by some Western military patients and travellers, as well as by many millions of developing country patients.

— The Western market *is* commercially interesting, but a slightly different product is needed for the developing country market. The additional R&D needed to create the developing country product is generally cheaper (as it can leverage commercial work already done) but the developing country market is still insufficient to offset even this reduced cost. Typical examples are vaccines for pneumonia, meningitis or HIV, which need to address developing country strains that are uncommon in Western patients with these diseases. Some veterinary products for Type III diseases that affect both humans and animals may also fall into this category, e.g. leishmaniasis treatments.

Non-commercial markets

These markets are too small to stimulate innovation by any firm. That is, any price point that covers R&D and normal commercial returns will still be too high for purchasers. Most Type III NDs fall into this category.

Markets for different firms

The key point to note in designing incentives for pharmaceutical R&D is that the attractiveness of a neglected disease market is *not determined by potential market size*, so much as by the balance between market size, R&D cost and risk, and the level of returns the pharmaceutical company normally aims for.

The size of a market does not only depend on the number of patients multiplied by their purchasing power, it also depends on the ability to cost-effectively access these patients. Thus, urban patients represent a more viable market than patients in remote rural areas; diseases that are regionally concentrated can be more attractive than those that are scattered globally; and countries with rapid marketing approval can be more attractive than those that take many months or even years to approve a product for use. Some product markets are also intrinsically less reliable, for instance HIV or cervical cancer vaccine markets can be at risk due to concerns in some sectors of society that such vaccines might encourage promiscuity.

R&D costs are similarly complex, depending on four key factors:

— Different diseases have very different R&D costs. Acute diseases can have clinical trials as short as 30 days, while chronic diseases may require trials of several years. The presence of surrogate markers of success for some diseases (e.g. hypertension, HIV) allows drug trials to be significantly shorter than for diseases like TB, where patients must be followed for years to determine a product's effectiveness. The state of science for a given disease also plays a crucial role: if aetiology, vectors, immune responses or targets are poorly understood (as with latent TB or Buruli ulcer), a pharmaceutical firm embarking on finding a new diagnostic or treatment runs a far higher risk of

failure than a firm developing a treatment for a disease such as hypertension or malaria, which is well understood.
— Different **products** have very different R&D costs and risks. Taking cost of failure into account, diagnostics have development costs in the $2 million to $30 million range, short development times (3-5 years) and face low regulatory hurdles. Drugs costing in the low hundreds of millions can take 7-12 years to develop and face higher regulatory requirements, while re-formulations or new fixed-dose combinations (FDC) of existing products can have particularly low risks and costs. Vaccines pose the greatest hurdles of all, costing hundreds of millions, spending up to 15 years in development and requiring manufacturing capacity upgrades, as well as trials in many thousands of patients[iii].
— Different **R&D stages** have very different costs and risks. Basic research has the highest scientific risk but the lowest cost, with risk decreasing and cost increasing as research moves into early development and later into clinical studies in humans. As an example, a late stage malaria vaccine can require two-year trials in 16,000 children and infants in half a dozen endemic countries, as well as the construction of a manufacturing plant. By contrast, early tests of a malaria vaccine can be conducted in 30 to 40 healthy adults in existing trial centres in high-income countries, with follow-up of a few weeks
— Different **companies** have very different cost structures. Multinational companies (MNCs) with a large global infrastructure have higher overheads than small Western-based smaller pharmaceutical and biotechnology companies (SMEs) with 30-40 staff. BRIC-based firms have significantly lower staff costs than Western firms, and may also have significant savings on physical infrastructure and clinical trial conduct. These firms also differ in terms of their minimum acceptable returns, with MNCs sometimes quoting a figure of $500-700m as the minimum market needed to justify R&D investment. Innovative developing country (IDC) firms, by contrast, can find even low-margin generic and international tender markets sufficiently attractive to justify production.

The interaction of these factors means that different neglected disease product areas represent less or more attractive markets for different firms. As shown in Table 3-1, many more areas are potentially commercial for IDC companies (technological capacity allowing) than for SMEs, and likewise for SMEs over MNCs. In brief, the only commercially interesting area for MNCs is HIV drug development, with pneumonia and rotavirus vaccine development for developing country use being borderline interesting[iv]. SME commercial interest extends to HIV drugs, diagnostics and vaccines, with TB markets being borderline interesting. IDC firms, by contrast, are active in HIV, TB and malaria diagnostics, FDCs and reformulations, but also find HIV, TB and malaria borderline commercially interesting. This division likely reflects their current capacity for novel drug and vaccine development and will very probably change as their pharmaceutical

---

[iii] For example, discovery and development costs of a novel TB drug have been estimated at US$115- 240 million, including cost of failure, while vaccine development from research and discovery through to registration has been estimated at US$200- 500 million, also including cost of failure, with other estimates being even higher.

[iv] Commercial is defined as independent industry activity driven by the market even in the absence of incentives. Borderline is defined as industry activity in the presence of incentives or charitable investment; or, in the case of SMEs, activity by 1-10 firms, with or without incentives.

Table 3-1. Markets for different firms

	DC Pneumonia vaccine	DC Rotavirus vaccine	HIV drugs	HIV diagnostics	HIV vaccines	TB vaccines	TB drugs	TB diagnostics	Malaria drugs	Malaria diagnostics	Malaria vaccines	NTDs
IDC firms												
Diagnostics				Y				?		Y		N
FDCs/reformulations			Y				Y		Y			N
Drugs novel			?				?		?			N
Vaccines novel	?	?			?	?					?	N
SME firms												
Diagnostics				Y				Y		~N		N
FDCs/reformulations			Y				N		?			N
Drugs novel			Y				?		?			N
Vaccines novel	?	?			Y	?					?	N
MNC firms												
Diagnostics				~N				~Y		N		N
FDCs/reformulations			Y				N		N			N
Drugs novel			Y				~N		N			N
Vaccines novel	?	?			N	N					N	N

Y=Commercial/ ~ = borderline/ N= non-commercial/ DC = Developing Country/ NTD = Neglected Tropical Disease/ IDC = Innovative Developing Country/

capability grows. Almost no firms find neglected tropical diseases (NTDs) commercially attractive, at least for human product development (veterinary activity is a different matter).

Incentives to stimulate pharma innovation

When markets are insufficiently attractive to generate products needed to achieve public health goals, governments often intervene to tip the cost-profit balance in favour of profit. They do so by deploying a range of incentives, with these aiming to either:

— Increase industry profits without cutting R&D cost and time. These approaches aim to generate increased revenue through creation of more sales or increased returns on sales (see Table 3-2); or

— Cut industry R&D cost, time and risk. These approaches aim to cut costs in order to tip the balance towards greater profits (see Table 3-2).

Many of these approaches are also in place —or have been proposed— as incentives for neglected disease pharmaceutical innovation. The main purpose of these incentives is to provide funds in the most efficient way, that is, to generate the greatest return for the least outlay. This means identifying which markets are attractive, borderline or unattractive for which industry sectors, and tailoring incentives accordingly. Attempting to make attractive markets out of markets that are currently unattractive to some developers is much more expensive and difficult than focusing on markets that are already attractive or borderline for those groups. It is also important to recognize that some markets will never be attractive to any developer, either because they are too small or because the science is too difficult and uncertain for the foreseeable future.

A second factor to take into account in designing incentives is whether they aim to generate 'industry-level' profits, or to accept a breakeven return or even a loss. A profit-focused approach is not feasible for non-commercial markets: it simply invites waste of public and philanthropic funding in an expensive uphill battle to increase returns and decrease costs to the extent needed to satisfy commercial groups. Although difficult, it is however possible to pursue a profit-focused approach for some borderline markets. The larger the Western market for a borderline disease, the greater the likelihood that a profit-focused approach will work (TB being a good example). Such an approach has the advantage of using market incentives to motivate more firms to pursue the desired R&D.

Profit-focused approaches are generally more expensive than 'breakeven' approaches, since public and philanthropic donors must fund the additional profit margin unless the incentive is designed to secure partial or full funding from Western consumers. The target firms may also factor in a risk premium due to the uncertainty of public and philanthropic funding. A final consideration in designing profit-based incentives is the nature of the firms they are targeting. It is very difficult indeed for public funders to match MNC profit expectations. In most cases an MNC will only become involved if it is willing to accept below-average returns. By contrast, IDC firms and SMEs are more likely to respond to profit-based incentives, since their expectations are likely to be more closely in line with the amounts that public and philanthropic donors are willing to pay.

Table 3-2. Incentives proposed for neglected disease markets (and OECD examples for comparison)

Approach		OECD example	Neglected disease example	Suitable for… B N
Policies to increase industry profits without altering R&D costs				
Increase demand/access	Use public funds to subsidise price to the consumer	PBS, NHS Medicaid	AMFm for malaria drugs (ACTs)	B
			AMC for pneumonia vaccines (GAVI co-payment) Health Impact Fund*	N
	Advertising	DTCA in the US	N/A for DCs as burden shifted to consumer	NOT SUITABLE
	Bulk purchase discounts (but if unit price is too low, this may not translate into increased industry revenues)	US Health insurance funds	AMFm TB Global Drug Facility UNICEF vaccines	B N
	Public procurement contracts (may or may not include bulk purchase discounts)	Project Bioshield	AMFm AMC	B N
Increase margins	Allow price premiums	US market (non-Medicaid) CONSUMER PAYS	Price premiums from W'n consumers and/or public funds: – PDP-FF (consumers and public) – AMC (public)	B N – less suitable as very expensive for the public

B: Borderline markets; N: Non-markets.

Table 3-2. Continuation

Approach	OECD example	Neglected disease example	Suitable for… B N
Policies to increase industry profits without altering R&D costs			
Increase margins	Increased patent/market life	Orphan drug legislation - CONSUMER PAYS Paediatric extension - CONSUMER PAYS	Western consumers cross-subsidise developing country users: – PRV on an unrelated commercial product – Orphan (market extension on neglected disease product in West)	B Not for B-adapted N - PRV yes/ Orphan No
	Prize payments (in addition to usual market sales)	InnoCentive X-Prize Foundation	InnoCentive (modest) Gates grand challenges TB diagnostic prize (Canada) Chagas disease prize fund KEI prizes	B N- Useable, but more expensive
Policies to decrease industry R&D time-costs to tip the balance towards greater profit			
Cut R&D costs	Streamlined regulation	Shift burden of proof balance from Phase III to Phase IV	Probably not safe given poor Phase IV in many DCs, so not recommended	B N

B: Borderline markets; N: Non-markets.

Table 3-2. Continuation

Policies to decrease industry R&D time-costs to tip the balance towards greater profit

Approach		OECD example	Neglected disease example	Suitable for... B N
	Streamlined development	Surrogate end-point for first HIV drugs EC Innovative Meds Initiative (pre-competitive shared development)	Open source (Synaptic Leap etc) Patent pools	B N
Cross-subsidize markets	Re-purposing existing drugs (R&D heavily subsidised by original R&D)	Every company when they can, e.g. Prozac for women's loss of libido FDA's Rare Disease Repurposing Database	Vet drugs developed for human use New neglected disease indication for an existing human drug	B N
R&D subsidies	Industry grants	SBIR programmes Orphan grants and fee waivers (small) DARPA CRADAs	Western SBIR programmes (very small) Developing country SBIR programmes, e.g. India's SIBRI Orphan (very small) PDPs Fund for R&D in neglected diseases (FRIND)	B N

B: Borderline markets; N: Non-markets.

Table 3-2. Continuation

Approach	OECD example	Neglected disease example	Suitable for... B N
Policies to decrease industry R&D time-costs to tip the balance towards greater profit			
Researcher grants	MRC, NIH etc	MRCs, NIH, WT Translation Awards — B N; PDPs; R&D Global Funds, R&D Treaty; Fund for R&D in neglected diseases (FRIND)	
Industry R&D tax breaks	UK R&D programme: 175% for SMEs, 130% for MNCs; Orphan tax breaks	UK neglected disease programme – 150% — B N	

B: Borderline markets; N: Non-markets.

However, unlike Western public health incentives, neglected disease approaches are not always designed to tip the balance towards profits. In some cases, they aim instead for a breakeven return (the 'no-profit/no loss' model) or even accept a loss. Although these non-profit activities may be conducted by many different sectors, for example industry, public research, or the activities of Product Development Partnerships (PDPs), they are invariably funded by public, philanthropic or corporate charitable funding.

These breakeven/loss-making approaches are suitable for both borderline and non-commercial markets. However, much larger incentives may be needed to reach the breakeven point for the latter, since, unlike borderline markets, there is limited or no opportunity for cross-subsidy from either R&D or markets related to a Western product. These approaches are also non-automatic, i.e. they require ongoing public or philanthropic funding, even to 100% in the case of some non-commercial diseases. If this funding ceases, the R&D also ceases.

Review of current incentives

It is clear from the above that no one incentive can be suitably sized for all diseases, developers and products. Failure to sufficiently tailor incentives to their target leads to the risk of overpay for lower-cost products and industry sectors —with the result that public funding crowds out industry investment— and under-pay for high-cost or risk products and high-cost industry sectors, resulting in failure of the incentive to stimulate the desired activity. Below, we review examples of key neglected disease R&D incentives to assess their suitability to a range of target disease areas and firms. All unattributed quotations are from interviews conducted by the author in 2010.

Incentives that increase or create profits

Affordable Medicines Facility – malaria (AMFm)

The AMFm aims to increase sales (use) of artemisinin combination therapies (ACTs) for malaria, and to protect both industry revenues and patient access by subsidizing the price to developing country patients. The AMFm purchase fund uses pooled demand to negotiate lower prices for effective anti-malarials with pharmaceutical producers, and makes these drugs more affordable for developing country buyers by underwriting their cost via a co-payment system. Funding for the co-payment scheme for the first two years (totalling US$225 million) has been provided by three public and philanthropic donors: UNITAID, the UK Government, and the Bill & Melinda Gates Foundation. The pilot program was launched in April 2009 in 11 countries[v], and will be independently evaluated in late 2011[1].

Purchase or procurement funds (the AMFm is only one example) are strongly supported by all industry sectors, being described as, "…the best signal" and "our preferred approach", particularly if the purchase commitments are contracted and long-term.

Such procurement funds are suited to all borderline and non-commercial disease markets for drugs, diagnostics and vaccines, since they increase the market for the former

---

[v] Benin, Cambodia, Ghana, Kenya, Madagascar, Niger, Nigeria, Rwanda, Senegal, Tanzania and Uganda.

and create a market for the latter where none previously existed. Caution needs to be exercised, however, in the case of procurement funds that do not include a price subsidy to patients, as the pressure to keep prices low can remove the profit incentive completely or encourage firms to cut corners in order to maintain margins.

Health Impact Fund (HIF)

The HIF proposal aims to increase access (sales) by converting non-markets into publicly-funded markets. Under the HIF proposal, a patented product is 'converted' into multiple low-priced generic equivalents through licensing agreements. The originator firm forgoes patent returns on a likely very small developing country market and is instead reimbursed from a donor fund in proportion to the increased sales (and health impact) of the cheaper generic version of its product. This provides increased patient access and new profits funded by public and philanthropic dollars[2]. The HIF could be used for any product but "is likely to be dominated by drugs and vaccines"[vi], at an estimated cost of around $6 billion per year. Around 10% of this funding is for a central group to analyse the on-the-ground health impact of each product in developing countries in order to determine the funding received by each company[2].

Companies reported mixed views on the HIF. Small companies described it as "very unattractive", since they would have to fund all R&D upfront in order to claim the eventual HIF reward post-marketing —most small firms simply do not have the resources to provide this level of funding for the decade or more of product development. Companies in general also expressed doubts about financial rewards based on health impact assessment, which they believed to be a risky approach: "…measuring impact is an inexact science— anything that introduces uncertainty is almost impossible to overcome from an incentive perspective". Nevertheless, many industry interviewees were interested in further exploration of the HIF, seeing it as a potential way to commercialise currently borderline or non-commercial disease areas.

The HIF is suited to both borderline and non-commercial market diseases, although it offers the greatest incentive for high-burden diseases such as malaria or helminth infections (with concomitantly high health impact payments), where fewer developers are competing for a share of the disease market.

Advance Market Commitment (AMC)

The AMC takes a similar approach to the AMFm, being designed to provide companies with secure profits and simultaneously subsidise developing country patient prices to protect access. However, in the case of the AMC, the international provider agency signs the purchase contract with companies *in advance* of the desired vaccine being successfully developed and registered. Under the AMC contract, the developer agrees to provide a certain volume of the finished product, and the agency agrees to pay a higher

---

vi Hollis A, Pogge T. The Health Impact Fund: making new medicines accessible for all (Incentives for Global Health, 2008) p.17.

price on an initial proportion of sales in return for a lower subsequent price[3]. This pricing structure was designed to provide firms with industry-level profits to incentivise them to conduct R&D and invest in the vaccine manufacturing plant needed in advance of successful registration. Public/philanthropic funds are used to subsidise the price to patients during the initial 'high price' period. An AMC is in place for pneumonia vaccines, administered by the Global Alliance for Vaccines and Immunisation (GAVI) and with a fund of $1.5 billion committed by public and philanthropic donors[4]. To date, 30% of this commitment has been allocated for 60 million vaccine doses per year from 2012 to 2023. New AMCs have been proposed for other vaccines (and occasionally for drugs).

An AMC is not attractive to all firms or for all products. While being a significant cost for public donors, the size of the price subsidy is far from matching normal MNC commercial vaccine returns. For instance, under the existing AMC contract, GSK and Pfizer could each receive around $1.3 billion over 10 years (this being pneumonia vaccine sales revenues plus the frontloaded price subsidy), averaging around $130 million per year. By contrast, in 2009, Merck's Rotateq (rotavirus) vaccine had sales of $522 million, slightly more than four times greater. MNCs advised that the public offering of a $1.5 billion AMC was "barely profitable for large companies", and that an AMC "would need to be substantially larger than $1.5 billion to support full product development". They noted, however, that AMCs "could steer existing R&D (for Western markets) towards the needs of DCs", for instance, end-stage development to include new developing country strains in existing vaccines, as was the case with the pneumonia vaccine AMC. AMCs are less attractive for small firms, which may prefer simple purchase commitments, but they can be attractive to IDC firms with lower profit expectations, lower cost structures and an interest in skilling-up for vaccine development and production.

As noted, AMCs are best suited to incentivising development of adapted vaccine products for borderline markets such as pneumonia, meningitis or rotavirus but are less suited to incentivising R&D of novel vaccines. For borderline vaccine markets where the same product is needed in the West and DCs (e.g. an HPV vaccine), the product will be developed with or without the AMC, so a simple purchase fund or price subsidy is more relevant. While theoretically suitable for non-market vaccines, in practice an AMC would be required to be very large to cover R&D time-costs (which in the case of non-commercial disease could not be cross-subsidised by R&D for a Western version of the product) and would thus probably be beyond the willingness of public donors. AMCs are poorly suited to incentivise drug R&D since, unlike vaccines, the drug market for a given disease is normally difficult to estimate, variable, and fragmented among many products and suppliers. Hence, contracting fixed AMC production and sales of any one product would be difficult both to undertake and to enforce, and they are unnecessary for diagnostics, as development costs and risks are too low to require complex advance contracting. AMCs are also unsuitable (and likely ineffective) for diseases where the basic science is weak or inexistent, for example to stimulate new investment in HIV or malaria vaccines.

Product Development Partnership Financing Facility (PDP-FF)

The proposed PDP-FF also aims to increase industry profits, in this case as a means to draw private capital into neglected disease R&D. The PDP-FF proposes selling bonds in private capital markets, using the funds raised by this exercise to support R&D of neglected disease products. Bond holders would be repaid from royalties on commercial sales in high- and middle-income countries and from donor-funded price premiums on sales in low-income countries. To reduce the risk to bond holders and allow the financing facility to borrow at low interest rates, it would back its borrowing with guarantees from donor governments and possibly foundations. The incentive is funded by Western consumers (who pay commercial price markups on the neglected disease product) and by donors, who pay price markups on behalf of developing country patients[5]. Initially designed to secure increased private funding for HIV, TB and malaria vaccine R&D, the proposed scope has been expanded to other product areas and neglected diseases (based either on existing classifications or a broader grouping that includes non-communicable and chronic diseases that disproportionately affect developing countries).

The PDP-FF is only suited to disease markets with some prospects of commercial returns, for example pneumonia, meningitis or TB (and some malaria products). It is less suitable for borderline areas with high scientific uncertainty, such as HIV or malaria vaccines, since failure to realise commercial returns would leave donors liable for substantial investor repayments. It is unsuitable for non-commercial diseases, even those with solid scientific underpinnings. Since these offer no hope of commercial returns, donors would effectively pay not only the developing country price premium on a successful product (similar to the AMC), but also the additional return to investors, so they would in this instance be better advised to pursue a direct purchase commitment.

Priority Review Voucher (PRV)

The PRV generates increased returns for the developer by awarding them a tradeable voucher for "priority regulatory review" of a *commercial* drug in return for registration of a 'new' neglected disease drug in the United States (although the drug may already have been registered and used elsewhere). Priority review of the commercial product allows a company to bring it to market faster, potentially resulting in many hundreds of millions of dollars of additional sales, particularly for 'blockbusters'[6]. It has been estimated that a reduction in the review time from 19.4 to 6.4 months for a drug receiving priority review could be worth US$322 million to developers[7]. The PRV is awarded on US registration of a neglected disease drug for one of the sixteen designated neglected diseases[vii], but does not require companies to manufacture or sell the product in DCs. The PRV has the attractive feature of being funded by US consumers, since it is the additional sales period on the commercial product that gives the voucher its value.

The PRV's value is particularly attractive for small firms with lower cost structures, such as SMEs and IDCs. These firms noted that the PRV was "a good match for the SME model"

[vii] TB, malaria, dengue, cholera, trachoma, leprosy, Buruli ulcer, fascioliasis, dracunculiasis, lymphatic filariasis, onchocerciasis, schistosomiasis, soil-transmitted helminthiasis and yaws. Two of the three kinetoplastid diseases are also included (sleeping sickness and leishmaniasis) but Chagas' disease, endemic in South America, is excluded, as is HIV/AIDS.

and "incentivises MNCs to partner with us and buyout our IP". However, some also noted their need for supplementary R&D grant funding as they did not have the internal resources to move projects forward to the point of either selling the IP or claiming the voucher. PRVs are less attractive for larger firms, for which the voucher value is less competitive with normal commercial returns, and whose overall R&D costs may be higher.

The PRV is suitable for drug development for both borderline and non-market areas, with one significant proviso: since the value of the reward is fixed, the PRV inadvertently provides the largest financial incentive to those who conduct the least R&D (e.g. US re-registrations of drugs already registered elsewhere; adaptations or re-purposing of existing drugs), and the lowest incentive to those who develop genuinely novel neglected disease drugs, as their R&D costs will eat up a significant proportion of the value of the reward. For instance, the first PRV was awarded for the anti-malarial Coartem, which had been registered and sold in more than 80 countries since 1999[8], but received a PRV in April 2009 for US registration, delivering a large benefit to its developer.

Orphan Drug Legislation (ODL)

ODL, as seen in Australia, the European Union, Japan and the United States of America, was designed to tip the cost-profit balance for rare[viii] non-commercial Western diseases by providing increased profits, generated through market exclusivity ranging from seven years in the United States to 10 years in Europe, accompanied by modest R&D subsidies. The market exclusivity is only valuable for products not already covered by patent protection for the length of this period, and where the value of the market exclusivity is greater than the cost of the R&D[6].

Orphan legislation is also sometimes considered a driver for neglected disease drugs, but is far less effective in this respect, since the key incentive (market exclusivity) is of very low value in Western orphan jurisdictions. This means developers only receive a financial return if they can keep their R&D costs below the already very small market value. As a result, two-thirds of neglected disease orphan approvals between 1985 and 2005 were drugs that required little or no investment in innovation, such as re-registrations of existing drugs, or adaptations and re-purposing of existing products[ix]. Most companies using orphan incentives for neglected diseases are very small, particularly for R&D that requires more than the most basic levels of innovation, as only very small firms with low cost structures can hope to make a profit from the neglected disease orphan incentive, and their efforts are concentrated on the most commercial of the borderline diseases, such as TB. As with the PRV, orphan legislation has the benefit that the additional industry returns are funded by Western consumers of the product.

In its current form, ODL is not suitable for incentivising neglected disease product development by any firms. The incentive could, however, be greatly improved by allowing reciprocal recognition of orphan neglected disease approval between stringent

---

[viii] Rare diseases are those with a prevalence of fewer than 5 cases per 10,000 inhabitants in Europe and fewer than 200,000 cases in the United States.

[ix] Unpublished internal analysis.

Western regulatory authorities, that is, approval by an authority in one Western juris-diction would confer automatic approval in other Western jurisdictions, and possibly also by the WHO Prequalification scheme, which approves drugs for developing coun-try use. The value of the orphan market would then be the collective value of the disease market in the US, Europe, Japan and Australia plus the global developing coun-try market —a situation much more likely to tip the cost-profit balance in favour of profits.

Approaches that decrease R&D time, cost and risk

Regulatory and development efficiencies

The opportunity cost of capital during the time a product is being developed repre-sents around 50% of its overall cost[9], with the value of the final market being much higher if it can be accessed today rather than in several years' time. Thus regulatory and develop-ment efficiencies offer the greatest potential of all R&D cost-cutting measures. These include modest measures to decrease time and cost (patent pooling[10,11], open source information sharing[12]), but the biggest time-cost savings are achieved through regulatory changes that allow products to be developed more quickly. Examples include the use of surrogate endpoints, such as CD4 counts for HIV drugs, and steps that allow trials to overlap rather than being conducted sequentially. For instance, the Critical Path to TB Drug Regimens (CPTR), created by the Global Alliance for TB Drug Development, the Critical Path Institute, and the Bill & Melinda Gates Foundation, could potentially reduce the time it takes to trial new combination TB treatments from as much as a quarter of a century to as little as six years. This represents removal of an almost insurmountable time-cost barrier, making TB drug development a far more feasible commercial prospect. Initial groups engaged in the CPTR include the US regulatory authority, the Food and Drug Administration (FDA), as well as several MNCs and some SMEs, including Johnson&Johnson, Sanofi-Aventis, Pfizer, AstraZeneca, GlaxoSmithKline, Bayer, Otsuka, Novartis, Sequella and Anacor Pharmaceuticals.

There are also regulatory pathways specifically aimed at expediting registration of neglected disease products for developing world use. For example, the European Medi-cines Agency's (EMA) Article 58 provides a regulatory review that developing country authorities can use to support more rapid review and approval by their own legisla-tures[13]. In theory, such a pathway should allow more rapid access to developing country markets, even if small, and thus assist in tipping the balance towards profit. In practice, however, Article 58 has barely been used by the industry, since its design requires firms to choose between developing country access expedited by Article 58 and access to more commercial European markets using traditional regulatory pathways. For most firms, the latter is a clear choice.

Despite issues with Article 58, all industry sectors interviewed rated regulatory and development efficiencies as the highest of all incentives, noting that, "the most immedia-tely effective incentive would be eliminating regulatory barriers". Such efficiencies are relevant to all neglected (and commercial) disease areas and products. However, to date there has been limited progress in or attention to them.

Re-purposing

A further approach is re-purposing of existing commercial drugs for neglected disease use. This is a highly cost-effective way to make neglected disease markets more attractive, since development costs can often be limited to end-stage human trials to establish efficacy and dose regimens for the new disease indication, resulting in major reductions in cost, risk and time to market. The FDA recently launched a Rare Disease Re-purposing Database (RDRD) to allow developers to identify opportunities to develop niche therapies that are already well-advanced through development, and that could have modest final development undertaken for use in a rare disease/orphan indication in the US.

Industry routinely uses re-purposing in commercial areas, and it was historically a common method of achieving new neglected disease drugs, particularly before the year 2000, when funding for neglected disease R&D was very low. Examples include the re-development of veterinary anti-helminthic drugs for human use, such as Mectizan (ivermectin) for onchocerciasis, Biltricide (praziquantel) for schistosomiasis, and Zentel (albendazole) for lymphatic filariasis. Instances where commercial drugs were extended for new neglected disease indications include Ambisome, developed for HIV and re-purposed for leishmaniasis; and the antibiotics moxifloxacin and gatifloxacin, now being re-developed for TB. Industry frequently turns to re-purposing when neglected disease incentives are undersized, as is the case with orphan drug legislation, and it is also highly likely as a response to fixed-value incentives such as the PRV.

Re-purposing is effective for drugs for both borderline and non-commercial markets, with the prospect of providing profits in the former and limiting losses in the latter. It is unsuitable for biologics such as vaccines.

R&D subsidies

Public R&D subsidies are in place in most Western countries, with the aim of cutting R&D costs in order to allow small markets to become profitable for developers. They are generally in the form of grants to academics, funding for government or public research institutions (e.g. National Institutes of Health (NIH), UK Medical Research Council), or grants for industry (e.g. orphan grants, small business innovation research (SBIR) grants). Many countries also provide tax breaks for companies conducting R&D, with some specifically including neglected disease provisions (e.g. the UK's 150% neglected disease R&D tax rebate for SMEs and large companies, or 16% tax credit for SMEs not making a profit).

Since 2000, a new source of R&D subsidies for industry has appeared in the form of Product Development Partnerships (PDPs)[11]. PDPs are not-for-profit product development groups that use donor grants to identify and fund development of promising neglected disease products in industry or academia. In 2007, PDPs received US$469 million, or roughly a quarter of all 'external' R&D funding for neglected diseases[x].

---

[x] Internal funding is granted by an organisation to its own bodies, for example NIH funding to the NIAID. External funding is funding granted by an organisation to another organisation, and is thus competitively available.

Nearly half of this (49%) was provided by the Gates Foundation, with a quartet of public funders (the US Agency for International Development, the UK Department for International Development, the Dutch Government and Irish Aid) providing a further 28%. In turn, PDPs funded a wide range of company-neglected disease activity, in particular MNC not-for-profit programmes, but also SMEs and IDC firms[14].

Several proposals for very large publicly-controlled R&D funds also exist, in particular the R&D Treaty, which proposes funding pharmaceutical development through a system of national and international grants, prizes, tax breaks and so forth, essentially replacing or running parallel to the IP system[15], and a range of proposals for similar but smaller global R&D funds for specific areas (e.g. neglected disease products only, or PDPs only).

All industry sectors strongly supported R&D subsidies (sometimes called 'push' funding, as opposed to 'pull' funding, which aims to increase the end return on investment), particularly for early-stage R&D. Typical responses were: "the best option combines both push and pull funding, and offers different incentives for early- and late-stage R&D", and, "pull funding is quite difficult as it doesn't fund the actual R&D – getting funding for this is now the rate-limiting step". Nevertheless, different sectors preferred different "push" approaches, with MNCs strongly disposed towards partnering with PDPs on development programmes, while SMEs preferred business grants or milestone payments that allowed them greater control. Tax breaks were not an appealing form of subsidy, being described by SMEs as unattractive (too little, too late) and by MNCs as irrelevant. Likewise, there was very limited industry interest in the R&D Treaty proposal, courtesy of its perceived anti-IP approach.

R&D subsidies are suitable for all sectors and products, and for both borderline and non-commercial R&D. They are vital for SMEs, and useful for MNCs seeking a breakeven outcome on their neglected disease R&D.

A new framework: matching incentives to products and developers

The brief review of incentives above shows that many of the existing and proposed neglected disease incentives are relatively blunt instruments. In some cases, for example the PRV, they offer the same return for borderline or non-commercial diseases and for simple US registration, as for a full product development programme over many years. Others are poorly sized for their target group, for instance the AMC as an incentive for MNCs to create novel neglected disease vaccines. It is also clear that government policy-makers diverge from developers in many areas, sometimes putting in place or supporting proposals that developers are unlikely to respond to (e.g. R&D tax breaks), while under-utilising approaches that are more likely to stimulate developers to invest in making new products for DCs (e.g. regulatory and development efficiencies). There is also a tendency for public policymakers to invest more time and money in incentives to support profits, such as the AMC or PRV, than in incentives to decrease industry R&D cost, time and risk, such as R&D grants for neglected diseases, funding for PDPs, or regulatory efficiencies. This continues despite industry need —and repeated calls— for the latter if they are to enter the neglected disease field.

Poor sizing and targeting of incentives can have at least two important negative results. The policy can end up having little or no impact, since developers ignore neglected disease incentives that are inappropriate to them, as is the case with Orphan Drug legislation, EMA Art. 58 and R&D tax breaks, all of which have barely been used to create neglected disease products. On the other hand, poorly designed incentives can result in developers being overpaid with public or consumer funds. For instance, revenues from the US orphan re-registration of thalidomide for leprosy topped the quarter-billion dollar per annum mark in 2004[16] due to the company's ability to leverage orphan status to market their product for an unrelated commercial disease.

We have therefore developed a framework that allocates the reviewed incentives based on the principles outlined above, in particular matching incentives to product and developer type for each disease market (see Table 3-3). In so doing, it becomes clear which approaches are most likely to be successful in delivering the desired products. Furthermore, it highlights areas where either no incentives are needed, or where new or adapted incentives will be needed. We emphasise that we are not endorsing these incentives (many have design flaws and difficulties as noted above[xi]) but simply noting which are best matched to the funding needs and commercial drivers that determine investment patterns.

If policymakers wish to extract greater returns from their neglected diseases R&D incentives, or to encourage more firms to enter currently neglected areas, they may wish to extend this analytical framework to other diseases, products and incentives in order to more closely tailor their policies and funding to the needs of industry innovators.

[xi] For a more detailed review of these incentives, see the 2010 Report of the WHO Expert Working Group on Innovative Financing for R&D, and the upcoming analyses by the Results 4 Development Institute in Washington.

Table 3-3. Matching incentives to products

Products	Market	Active Companies	Incentives for MNCs	Incentives for SMEs	Additions/exceptions
HIV drugs	Yes	MNCs SMEs	No incentives needed: Products being made already (Commercial drivers)		If DC adaptations needed, will need additional incentives e.g. DC suitable diagnostics/paediatric ARV formulations
HIV diagnostics	Yes	SMEs IDCs	Issues to adress are:		
HIV vaccines	Yes	SMEs	— IP/price/access (esp. MNC and SME)		
HIV drug FDCs	Yes	IDCs SMEs?	— Capacity building for IDC firms		
TB drug FDCs	Yes	IDCs	— Regulatory quality (some DC)		
Malaria drug FDCs	Yes	IDCs			
Malaria diagnostics	Yes	IDCs			
Pneumonia, rotavirus and meningitis vaccines (DC adaptation)	Borderline	MNCs	Public procurement R&D subsidies AMC HIF PDP-FF?		
		SMEs		Public procurement R&D subsidies PDP-FF	
HIV vaccines (DC adaptation)	Borderline	SMEs		Public procurement R&D subsidies	PDP-FF less suited for HIV vaccines - ideal for pneumo/rota/meningitis vaccines; diagnostics; repurposed products

Table 3-3. Continuation

Products	Market	Active Companies	Incentives for MNCs	Incentives for SMEs	Additions/exceptions
HIV diagnostics (DC adaptation)	Borderline	MNCs	Public procurement R&D subsidies PDP-FF?		
TB diagnostics (DC adaptation)	Borderline	MNCs	Public procurement R&D subsidies PDP-FF?		
	Borderline	SMEs		Public procurement R&D subsidies PDP-FF Prizes	
NTD drugs – Leishmaniasis drugs – Anti-helminthic drugs with vet overlap	Borderline/No	SMEs?		R&D subsidies PRV Public procurement Re-purposing PDP-FF	
TB drugs	Borderline	SMEs		R&D subsidies PRV Public procurement Re-purposing PDP-FF	
TB vaccines	Borderline	SMEs		Public procurement R&D subsidies PDP-FF	

Table 3-3. Continuation

Products	Market	Active Companies	Incentives for MNCs	Incentives for SMEs	Additions/exceptions
Malaria vaccines	Borderline	SMEs		Public procurement, R&D subsidies	Not PDP-FF due to scientific uncertainty
Malaria drugs	Borderline	SMEs		Public procurement, R&D subsidies, PRV, Re-purposing, PDP-FF	
Malaria FDCs	Borderline	SMEs		Public procurement, R&D subsidies, PDP-FF	PRV would be substantial overpay for FDC development, so not recommended
NTD vaccines	No	All	Public procurement, R&D subsidies, HIF	Public procurement, R&D subsidies	The HIF is particularly attractive for non-commercial diseases
NTD drugs (see exceptions above)	No	All	Public procurement, R&D subsidies, Re-purposing, HIF	Public procurement, R&D subsidies, PRV, Re-purposing	
NTD diagnostics	No	All	Public procurement, R&D subsidies	Public procurement, R&D subsidies, Prizes	
Malaria drugs	No	MNCs	Public procurement, R&D subsidies, Re-purposing, HIF, PDP-FF?		

Table 3-3. Continuation

Products	Market	Active Companies	Incentives for MNCs	Incentives for SMEs	Additions/exceptions
Malaria drug FDCs	No	MNCs	Public procurement R&D subsidies HIF		
Malaria diagnostics	No	MNCs	Public procurement R&D subsidies PDP-FF?		
	No	SMEs		Public procurement R&D subsidies Prizes PDP-FF	
Malaria vaccines	No	MNCs	Public procurement R&D subsidies HIF		
HIV vaccines	No	MNCs	Public procurement R&D subsidies HIF PDP-FF?		
TB vaccines	No	MNCs	Public procurement R&D subsidies HIF		
TB drugs	No	MNCs	Public procurement R&D subsidies Re-purposing HIF PDP-FF?		
TB drug FDCs	No	SMEs		Public procurement R&D subsidies	PRV would be substantial overpay por FDC development, so not recommended

REFERENCES

1. The Global Fund to Fight AIDS, TB and Malaria (GFATM): Introduction to the Affordable Medicines Facility – malaria. Available at: http://www.theglobalfund.org/content/pressreleases/pr_090417_Factsheet.pdf (accessed 8 November 2010).
2. Hollis A, Pogge T, et al. The Health Impact Fund: Pay-for-Performance (WHO Expert Working Group Submission 2009). Available at: http://www.who.int/phi/HIF.pdf (accessed 8 November 2010).
3. Light D. Advanced Market Commitments: Current Realities and Alternate Approaches: HAI Paper Series. 2009. Available at: http://www.haiweb.org/31032009/27%20Mar%202009%20AMC%20Current%20Realities%20&%20Alternate%20Approaches%20FINAL.pdf (Accessed 8 November 2010).
4. IHP - Taskforce on Innovative Financing for Health Systems: Raising and Channeling Funds. Working Group 2 report (2009). Available at: http://www.internationalhealthpartnership.net/CMS_files/userfiles/090817%20WORKING_GROUP_2(1).pdf (accessed 8 November 2010).
5. IAVI (2009). Financing the Accelerated Development of Vaccines for AIDS, TB, and Malaria: Design of the PDP Financing Facility and an Analysis of Its Feasibility (a Report to Aeras, IAVI, and MVI). Available at: http://healthresearchpolicy.org/sites/healthresearchpolicy.org/files/PDPFF%20financing%20vaccines%20for%20AIDS,%20TB,%20and%20malaria.pdf (accessed 8 November 2010).
6. Grabowski H, Ridley D, Moe J. Priority Review Vouchers to encourage innovation for neglected diseases. 2008. Available at: http://www.law.harvard.edu/programs/petrie-flom/workshops_conferences/2008_workshops/Grabowski.pdf (accessed 8 November 2010).
7. Ridley DB, Grabowski HG, Moe JL. Developing drugs for developing countries. Health Affairs. 2006, 25:313-24.
8. Novartis media release. September 15, 2008. Available at: http://www.novartis.com/newsroom/media-releases/en/2008/1251164.shtml. Accessed 2 November 2010
9. Di Masi JA, Hansen RW, Grabowski HG. The price of innovation: new estimates of drug development costs. Journal of Health Economics. 2003;22:151-85.
10. UNITAID. Proposals for New and Innovative Sources of Funding Medicines Patent Pool. 2009. Available at: http://www.who.int/phi/UNITAID.pdf (accessed 8 November 2010).
11. IFPMA Submission to the Public Hearing on Proposals for R&D Financing. Available at: http://www.who.int/phi/IFPMA.pdf (accessed 8 November 2010).
12. Everts S. Open-Source Science - Online research communities aim to unite scientists worldwide to find cures for neglected diseases. Chemical and Engineering News. 2006; 84(30):34-5. Available at: http://pubs.acs.org/cen/index.html (accessed 8 November 2010).
13. Pelfrene E. Article 58: A route to scientific opinion. EMEA; 2008. Available at: http://www.kaisernetwork.org/health_cast/uploaded_files/Article_58_A_Route_to_Scientific_Adoption_Eric_Pelfrene_5.6.08%5B1%5D.pdf (accessed 8 November 2010).
14. Moran M, Guzman J, Ropars AL, Illmer A. The role of Product Development Partnerships in research and development for neglected diseases. International Health. 2010;2(2). Available at: http://www.internationalhealthjournal.com/article/S1876-3413(10)00026-4/abstract (accessed 8 November 2010).
15. Health Action International (HAI). Response to the Expert Working Group on Alternative Financing. 2009. Available at: http://www.who.int/phi/HAI.pdf (accessed 8 November 2010).
16. Celgene media release, January 27, 2005. Available at: http://ir.celgene.com/phoenix.zhtml?c=111960&p=irol-newsArticle_Print&ID=667281&highlight=.(Accessed 2 November 2010).

CHAPTER 4

When patents are not enough: supplementary incentives for pharmaceutical innovation

Aidan Hollis

Introduction

Patents have proven to be an exceptionally effective mechanism for motivating innovation. A patent gives a firm the right to apply to the courts to enforce exclusive rights to the patented invention for a fixed period of time. The particular strength of the system is that patents offer a reward correlated with the value that consumers obtain from the product. Firms make decisions to invest in innovation based on their own information about the probability of success and the costs of research, as well as the expected value of the patent. The problem addressed in this paper relates to situations where for some reason the value of the patent reward is relatively low compared to the social value created by the innovation: that is, where the *appropriability* of social value is low. In these cases, firms will fail to invest in innovation even though its value to society is high.

There are a number of reasons why appropriability of a patent may be low. The first arises when the patent is ineffective at preventing competition, which can occur for various reasons, as discussed below. The second is that the market in which the innovation is to be employed is hampered by government-imposed distortions and inefficiencies. And third, there is the special case in which market value itself may poorly reflect social value.

In most industries, firms use a variety of mechanisms to appropriate value from invention, including patents, trade secrets, early entry and trademarks (Cohen, Nelson and Walsh, 2000). In pharmaceutical markets, however, patents take on an especially important position because of the high degree of substitutability between branded and generic products, which means that there is little protection other than the patent. This paper focuses particularly on pharmaceutical markets.

After discussing reasons for low appropriability, this chapter addresses some solutions, focusing on the Health Impact Fund (HIF) proposal (Hollis and Pogge, 2008). The HIF is sometimes seen as relevant chiefly for neglected diseases, although as discussed below, the proposal offers solutions to a much wider set of problems.

The reasons for low appropriability

Competition

In many cases, patents are not an effective tool for firms to capture profits from an invention – and indeed Cohen, Nelson and Walsh (2000) find that many firms outside the pharmaceutical and chemical industries do not view patents as a particularly effective tool for protecting innovation. There are a number of problems.

First, patents are time-limited, and so cannot prevent competition beyond 20 years. Most drugs take so long in clinical trials and approval that they obtain only 10-12 years of exclusivity. For some drugs, the time of protection granted by patents may be much shorter, resulting in weak incentives to continue investments in clinical trials. It is equally undesirable that the time-limited nature of patents results in strong incentives to rush through clinical trials, which need to be just good enough to attain regulatory approval. Firms may as a result set up clinical trials to examine the effectiveness of a drug over the course of a few weeks, even though they expect the product to be consumed for months or even years.

Second, patents can often be "invented around". In pharmaceutical markets, when a successful drug is introduced, there will often be a series of "me-too" or "follow-on" drugs that mimic the pioneer drug's action. For example, following the discovery of the effectiveness of Viagra, and its market potential, other similar drugs were brought to market. Lichtenberg and Philipson (2002) show that competition from drugs in the same therapeutic class costs innovators more than the competition from generics after patent expiry. While in many cases me-too drugs are simply the natural outcome of simultaneous research programs, in other cases they are explicitly the result of an intentional imitative research program (Garnier, 2008). Such me-too drugs may decrease the expected sales of the pioneer, and in addition lead to competitive marketing. Evidently, such marketing may be privately profitable for the firm, but to the extent that it reflects only competition for market share, it does little to generate real benefits for society. Such competition for market share may even hurt real innovation, since the pioneer drug in a market must also engage in costly competitive marketing.

Third, patents often provide no effective protection if the innovation is a new use, rather than a new molecule. For example, a discovery that high doses of a generic statin can effectively treat Alzheimer's Disease would be of enormous value but would not enable any firm to earn much money, since the patent could not be used to prevent consumers from using statins for this purpose. Since new uses need to be demonstrated through costly clinical trials, there is likely to be an underinvestment in this kind of research. Syed (2009) offers an overview of these points as well as the intellectual history relating the problems of ensuring incentives for innovation in the face of ineffective protection from competition.

Distorted and inefficient markets

If the market in which an innovation is to be used is itself distorted or broken, the social value of an innovation may fail to be realized, or may not be able to be appropriated.

Pharmaceutical markets are arguably among the least well functioning of all markets, because of informational constraints and insurance. These two distortions are extraordinarily powerful. Drugs are specialized products, dispensed only under prescription of a doctor. Unlike other markets in which consumers make choices based on their own preferences, drugs are chosen, based on expert knowledge, by someone other than the consumer. In addition, because drugs can be costly, there is widespread insurance coverage. Thus, the consumer neither chooses nor pays for the drug she consumes, which naturally and inevitably distorts choices. Price, for example, does not feature in the decision of the insured consumer or the prescribing doctor. At the same time, the insurer lacks detailed information about the patient's characteristics and situation, so while the insurer may be interested in price, it cannot weigh price against the demand for the product.

The response of many governments to pharmaceutical market distortions has been to apply price controls, or to limit the catalog of drugs that are reimbursed by the insurance plan. Governments often, in these circumstances, look for the most cost-effective drugs to fit within a given budget. While responsive to short-term fiscal requirements, this approach is not likely to create strong incentives for innovation.

Thus, pharmaceutical markets are exceptionally distorted in a variety of ways, and likely to be inefficient in ensuring that high-value innovations are appropriately rewarded.

Social value greater than market value

Pharmaceutical markets are also characterized by failures in market value that occur even without government intervention. There are at least four general problems. First, many diseases have important externalities relating to infectiousness. Vaccines, for example, protect not only the individual who is vaccinated, but others who are exposed to that individual. However, in valuing the vaccine, the individual is likely to consider chiefly the benefit to himself, rather than the social benefit created by reduced infection of others.

Second, many markets for pharmaceuticals are characterized by convex demand curves, especially in developing countries. The reason for this is that the willingness to pay for a drug is highly correlated with income – individuals will, for example, be willing to pay anything for a drug that saves their life. And in many developing countries, the income distribution highly unequal. As a result, a monopolist may have difficulty in appropriating the economic value of the market by choosing a single price. As a rule, the more equal willingness to pay across consumers, the more value a monopolist can extract. In markets with high income inequality, appropriability will be low (Flynn, Hollis, and Palmedo, 2009). While price discrimination could in principle address this problem, it is generally difficult to charge very different prices within the same geographic market.

Third, in many cases a given drug has multiple uses, often with different medical value. For example, many cancer drugs are used to treat different forms of cancer, and have different effectiveness across different indications. However, the firm may be unable to set price according to the use. It is evident why this is a problem: consider a drug that has a life-saving use, for which 10 individuals (or insurers) are willing to pay up to $100,000.

It also has an alternative use for soothing indigestion, for which 100,000 individuals are willing to pay up to $10 each. There is one million dollars in value available in each use, but it is not possible for the firm to effectively exploit both markets: either it prices the drug high, and loses the indigestion market, or it prices low, without really obtaining the value in the life-saving market. Pricing low, while leaving more consumer surplus available to buyers, leads to incomplete appropriation of social value and hence inadequate incentives for investment in the clinical trials for the product. This problem is another variant of the convex demand curve, but here the convexity depends on different uses rather than different incomes.

Finally, many consumers have very low ability to pay even for life-saving drugs. One approach to this is to assume that the value of a person who is unwilling to pay $100 for a drug that will save his life must be less than $100. However, in this situation it is much more likely that the individual simply does not have $100, even if it will save his life. The poor often live with no or little reserve for occasions when they are sick, resulting in delayed or incomplete treatment, or no treatment at all. This point is sometimes awkward for economists, who are accustomed to thinking of value in terms of willingness to pay (Viscusi and Aldy, 2003). When we value health in dollars, we will find that the poor value health less than the rich. But this does not mean that the poor value health in itself less than the rich: it means that they have a higher marginal utility of income (or of "other goods"). This problem is aggravated by deficient credit markets in poor countries, where a sick person will have difficulty borrowing against anticipated future income in order to pay for life-saving drugs today.

The last problem could be summarized in this way: economic value to a seller of drugs is denominated in dollars; but the value of a person's life to himself may not be well described in dollars. This does not mean that we should spend "whatever it takes" to extend life, but it does create problems. Our economic system uses economic value to allocate resources, but this is not the only source of value, nor should it be. The result of this problem is that there are numerous diseases that inflict great harm on humanity, but do not present an appealing target for pharmaceutical companies because most of the victims are relatively poor. These so-called "neglected diseases" are in some cases extremely important: tuberculosis leads to enormous suffering and millions of deaths, but since it is prevalent chiefly among the poor, the commercial interest in addressing it is not strong.

Solutions

I have presented three general reasons for the existence of gaps in the incentives provided by patents: insufficient protection from competition, dysfunctional markets for innovative goods, and failures in market value. What are the solutions?

Data Exclusivity

Data exclusivity is a relatively recent innovation in protecting innovative drugs. Essentially, data exclusivity grants an innovator firm a period of several years during which no generic firm can enter on the basis of clinical trial data presented to the regulatory authority for the purpose of approval. In principle, a generic firm that wished to produce the same product could work around the data exclusivity by conducting its own clinical trials, but in practice such trials are extremely costly and time consuming. Furthermore, such firms would likely fail to obtain ethics approval. Data exclusivity has varying durations in different countries, ranging from five years in the US to 10 years in Europe. Biologic drugs in the US can obtain 12 years.

As Eisenberg (2003-4) has observed, data exclusivity can help to address the problem that arises when a new drug is for some reason unable to use patent protection. For example, clinical trials might take so long that the patents obtained based on early research expire before the firm can benefit from them, i.e. the problem of time-limited patents is severe. Data exclusivity does not address any of the other problems discussed above.

Government funding of research

Governments invest an enormous amount of money in support of basic research at universities and elsewhere, and much of this research is extremely important in enabling inventions of significant commercial value. Such support can help to address many of the problems mentioned above. In cases of basic research, where commercial use of the invention is not likely within the 20-year patent life, government funding is essential. In cases of imperfect markets, government funding can also play an important role.

Unfortunately, governments also face serious problems in allocating research expenditures optimally and then ensuring effective use of the invention, and we rarely see governments bring a drug through from research to regulatory approval. The problems of allocating research expenditures become particularly severe at the clinical trials stage, as the cost of Phase III trials is typically in the tens of millions of dollars. While governments are able to direct such expenditures, the decision-making process becomes problematic when substantial risks are involved. For example, Pfizer allegedly spent nearly one billion dollars on the clinical development of its drug torcetrapib, mostly on Phase III trials[i]. Ultimately, the drug was unsuccessful. What politician would be willing to support such expenditures, given the risk of failure? Governments generally lack a process for evaluating major expenditures on clinical trials, and the political environment makes it difficult for most governments to engage in major expenditures laden with risk.

Foundation funding of research

Philanthropic organizations such as the Bill & Melinda Gates Foundation have a different structure of decision-making that may enable some risk-taking. They can therefore solve some of the problems of funding important but risky research. Indeed, these

---

[i] Alex Berenson and Andrew Pollock, "Pfizer Shares Plummet on Loss of a Promising Heart Drug". *New York Times:* 5 December 2006.

foundations have played a leading role in supporting "product-development partner-ships", which are focused on developing and testing new drugs for neglected diseases. Governments have been able to contribute to this effort by participating alongside as part-funders, so that each government has been able to diffuse some political risk by supporting a portfolio of projects.

The chief difficulty with philanthropy is ensuring that there is enough financial capacity. The Gates Foundation has made a very large impact by substantially increasing the level of financial support, such that it is now funding approximately half the total expenditures of product development partnerships (Moran et al. 2010). Some have questioned whether this approach is sustainable (Mossialos et al., 2010).

The Health Impact Fund proposal

This section is merely intended as a summary of the Health Impact Fund (HIF) proposal, which has been described in greater detail by Hollis and Pogge (2008). Key contributors to the core idea of a fixed fund with rewards shared on the basis of social benefit include Michael Abramowicz (2002) and James Love and Tim Hubbard (2007). The HIF is essentially a sophisticated prize mechanism that uses competition based on measured health benefits to set the amount of the prize. As Gallini and Scotchmer (2001) argue, a system of prizes is the best possible mechanism for stimulating innovation "if the size of the prize could be linked to the social value" of the innovation. This is exactly what the HIF attempts to do.

The basic idea of the HIF is that governments would collectively fund a fixed reward pool every year. Firms with an innovative pharmaceutical product could register the product with the HIF, in which case they would obliged to sell the product globally at the cost of production, or to license it for generic production. In exchange, the firm would become eligible to collect rewards from the HIF, with each firm obtaining rewards based on its share of the total health impact generated by all registered products, for a period of ten years. Thus, in a given year, if the reward pool were $6bn, and a firm's products were responsible for 10% of the total measured health impact assessed for all registered products, the firm would earn reward payments of $600m that year. Health impact would be assessed based on the incremental change in health outcomes due to the intro-duction of the registered drug, compared to a baseline of practice standards established before the drug was introduced. To allow for comparability across products and coun-tries, health impact would be expressed in terms of "quality-adjusted life-years" or QALYs.

Without going into all the details of how the assessment of health impact would operate, the key points to notice about the HIF proposal in this context include how it addresses the problems discussed above.

First, it evades the time-limited nature of patents by starting the reward clock *following* market approval —in the same way as data exclusivity— rather than at the time some preliminary patent is filed. Even if patents expire and other firms are able to compete during the 10-year reward period, the HIF would pay rewards based on assessed health impact of the aggregate sales of the registered product, regardless of the seller.

Second, while the HIF does not prevent competition from me-too products, it does not encourage such competition either. The incentives to register me-too drugs in the HIF are weak, since the incremental health benefit of those products tends to be small. Thus the HIF would not remove all incentive to engage in the development of imitative products, but would help to restructure incentives so that pioneer products were rewarded in proportion to their benefits.

Third, the HIF could be set up to reward new uses of existing molecules. Hollis and Pogge (2008) propose that firms demonstrating new uses of existing drugs should be eligible for rewards for five years only, since the risks are much smaller. In such a case, the registrant would obtain rewards based on the total benefit of the product in the new use, regardless of the supplier of the product.

Fourth, the HIF could play a significant role in addressing some of the problems relating to dysfunctional markets. Because the HIF would require drugs to be priced at the cost of production —essentially the generic price— the issue of price controls would generally not arise, and governments would have little incentive to reduce the use of a registered product in order to meet a budget constraint.

Fifth, the HIF would directly deal with the problems created by poor correlation between social values and willingness to pay. With respect to infectious diseases, the HIF's measure of health impact could naturally be designed to model a reduction in community infection rates when an individual is vaccinated. The health impact of a vaccination consists of the protection conferred upon on the individual and the reduced transmission to others, and the HIF could explicitly include this externality when calculating the reward due.

In cases of convex demand stemming from extreme income inequalities in a country, the HIF's mandated low pricing of registered drugs would facilitate a high uptake, while the cost of funding the HIF would likely be borne according to income. Thus, higher income individuals would contribute more to funding rewards, but this would not occur through high prices that would block access for the poor.

If a product had different uses, the HIF could adjust rewards to account for that. For example, if a product had a very high-value use among a small number of individuals, and a less valuable use among many individuals, the company could sell to all at a low price, but rewards would be calculated based on the estimated health benefits across the two groups. So the company need not sacrifice profits by selling at a price that is reasonable for the low-benefit use, and it need not sacrifice volume by selling only to the high-value consumers at a high price.

Finally, the HIF would not distinguish between people according to willingness to pay when calculating health benefit. Thus, extending the life of a poor person would represent a profit opportunity for registrants just as attractive as extending the life of a rich person. This would create incentives for firms to develop drugs that would be used chiefly to treat people in developing countries. It would also motivate companies to invest in making those drugs available, as the companies would be rewarded based on assessed health outcomes. Evidently, a firm that is compensated on a non-profit basis for supplying drugs to people in poor countries has little motivation to actually bother supplying. In contrast, the HIF would reward companies for improving health among the poor (as among the wealthy), and so companies would be incentivized to engage in the kinds of activities that are essential to making drugs available, such as obtaining timely regulatory approval.

One way of summarizing the HIF proposal is that pharmaceutical innovation that is therapeutically valuable, but commercially unattractive under our current systems, could be suitably rewarded. As such, the HIF is essentially designed to fill the gaps in the patent system that arise from the problems described above.

The HIF proposal depends crucially on the ability to measure health impact in a credible way. The patent system resolves the problem of setting rewards by granting a temporary monopoly on the use of the invention. Thus, the reward to the firm is related to the market value of the invention, insofar as it is determined through a market process, which means it typically depends on unobservable consumer valuations and preferences. Consequently, the HIF in some ways requires an artificial measure of value.

This construct, artificial though it may be, is nevertheless plausible for a number of reasons. First, where pharmaceuticals are concerned, consumer valuations and preferences are not so important as in other markets because governments or insurers often set the price based on considerations of expected health impact in any case. And second, for those pharmaceuticals designed principally to improve health, a measure of health impact can reasonably capture the value of the product in an appealing way, and one which is consistent with intuitions on the value of health and life.

Since the HIF system requires the ability to measure value without reference to price, the methodology is not readily generalizable. Hollis (2007) suggests some other industries in which the approach could perhaps be applied.

Summary

The patent system has been remarkably productive over the years, and this suggests that changes should be applied tentatively and gradually. However, patents are merely one instrument in the range of possible mechanisms for supporting investment in innovation. Government and foundation support of research has been —and continues to be— crucial, chiefly through direct funding of research into areas thought to be important and potentially productive.

The Health Impact Fund proposal can be seen as a gap-filling mechanism that identifies and automatically fills the patent system's shortcomings as regards new medicines —and new uses for old medicines— that are likely to have real therapeutic value but little commercial value.

REFERENCES

Abramowicz M. Perfecting patent prizes. Vanderbilt Law Review. 2003;56(1):114-236.
Cohen W, Nelson R, Walsh J. Protecting their intellectual assets: appropriability conditions and why U.S. manufacturing firms patent (or not). NBER WP. 2000;7552.
Eisenberg R. Lecture: Patents, Product Exclusivity, and Information Dissemination: How Law Directs Biopharmaceutical Research and Development. Fordham Law Review. 2003-4;72:477.
Flynn S, Hollis A, Palmedo M. An Economic Justification for Open Access to Essential Medicine Patents in Developing Countries. J Law Med Ethics. 2009;37(2):184-208.
Garnier JP. Rebuilding the R&D Engine in Big Pharma. Harvard Bus Rev. 2008;86(5):68-76.

Hollis A, Pogge T. The Health Impact Fund: Making New Medicines Accessible for All. Incentives for Global Health. 2008. New York.

Hollis A. Incentive Mechanisms for Innovation. University of Calgary: IAPR Technical Paper TP-07005; 2007.

Lichtenberg F, Philipson T. The dual effects of intellectual property regulations: within- and between-patent competition in the U.S. pharmaceuticals industry. J Law Econ. 2002;XLV:643-72.

Love J, Hubbard T. The Big Idea: Prizes to Stimulate R&D for New Medicines. Chic Kent Law Rev. 2007;82(3):1519-54.

Moran M, Guzman J, Ropars AL, Illmer A. The role of Product Development Partnerships in research and development for neglected diseases. Int Health. 2010;2:114-22.

Mossialos E, et al. 2010 Policies and incentives for promoting innovation in antibiotic research. Geneva: World Health Organization; 2010.

Syed T. Should a Prize System for Pharmaceuticals Require Patent Protection for Eligibility? Incentives for Global Health. Discussion Paper #2; 2009.

Viscusi WK, Aldy J. The Value of a Statistical Life: A Critical Review of Market Estimates Throughout the World. J Risk Uncertain. 2003;27(1):5-76.

CHAPTER 5

The Contribution of the United States, Europe and Japan in Discovering New Drugs: 1982-2003

Henry Grabowski

Introduction

In an article published in *Health Affairs* in 2006, Grabowski and Wang (G&W) examined trends in the introduction of new chemical entities (NCEs) worldwide from 1982 to 2003[1]. Although there is a well documented decline over time in total worldwide introductions, we found various quality indicators such as the number of global, first-in-class, biotech and orphan drugs exhibited more positive trends. U.S. headquartered firms also assumed a strong leadership position in terms of being the initial introducers of the most novel compounds including first-in-class, biotech and orphan drugs.

In this paper, I provide a complementary analysis to our earlier paper by focusing on the drug discovery stage across each of these regions. Multinational firms perform research and develop new drugs in several locations. Firms also enter partnering and licensing agreements involving new drug candidates, so the nationality of a firm introducing a product is often different from the one where the drug was invented and initially developed. There is also a well-defined and studied "market for innovation" in pharmaceuticals[2]. This is especially true in the biotech industry which has been the source of many novel products over the past two decades.

I utilize information contained in patent data to establish the region of discovery for all the first-in-class, biotech, global and orphan compounds in the G&W sample. These data show that R&D labs located in the U.S. have discovered more products in these categories than R&D labs based in Europe or Japan. U.S. leadership also has increased over time. These findings are consistent with other studies using different samples and indicators of drug discovery by countries and geographical regions.

In the next section, I summarize prior literature and discuss the rationale for utilizing first-in-class, biotech, global and orphan drugs as measures of drug quality. In the following sections, I present the empirical findings on the location of pharmaceutical discoveries in the United States, Europe and Japan for each of these drug quality measures. A subsequent section also considers several issues surrounding an analysis of R&D

productivity by region by Light that utilizes our data on new drug introductions[3]. The final section offers some observations on the policy implications of the analyses on international competitiveness undertaken here and in related studies.

Drug quality measures in the prior literature

In examining international data on innovative performance, various scholars and research organizations historically examined different output and input measures, such as new drug introductions, patent counts, and research and development expenditures[4]. While these provide nice aggregate quantitative measures, they do not capture the quality of introductions over time or how quality indexed introductions compare across countries.

A quality-oriented index that began receiving attention by scholars in the 1980s was the concept of consensus or global new chemical entities (NCEs)[5]. Global NCEs are defined as new drugs introduced into a majority of the world's leading drug markets. Several scholars noted that a large percentage of drug introductions historically were introduced into one or a few closely related countries. Global NCEs capture important therapeutic advances from a medical perspective as well as drugs that address significant market opportunities. In this regard, Grabowski (1989) found that although there were over 50 annual NCEs introduced internationally from the 1970s through 1983, only 24 percent of these were introduced into a majority of the world's largest markets.

In my study with Richard Wang, we considered global introductions as one index of drug quality, but developed some alternative measures that reflect other specific quality attributes. We gave particular attention to drug novelty or first-in-class drugs. In addition, we examined trends in and sources of biotech drugs and orphan compounds given that these entities often provide therapeutic advances for illnesses and disabilities with substantial unmet medical needs.

Sample Scope and Definitions in Grabowski and Wang's Analysis

The current analysis builds on Grabowski and Wang's sample and methodology to examine the country of discovery. In this section, a brief summary of the underlying data source is provided. Using the new Product Focus database (IMS Health Incorporated, Fairfield, Conn.), Grabowski and Wang identified all NCEs first introduced worldwide between 1982 and 2003. The database reports all drug launches in 68 countries. IMS Health defines NCEs based on the first international launch of a new active substance, including both new chemical entities and new biological products (specifically recombinant proteins and recombinant vaccines).

The definition of globe introductions in the Grabowski and Wang study considers dissemination in the G7 countries (Canada, France, Germany, Italy, Japan, the United Kingdom and the United States). We defined global NCEs as those introduced in a majority (at least four) of the G7 countries. These countries are the world's seven largest pharmaceutical markets.

We also identified the first NCE in a therapeutic class (first-in-class drugs). Therapeutic class is defined as the unique combination of the five-digit Uniform System of Classification (USC) and the four-level Anatomical Therapeutic Classification (ATC) system. We used the National Disease and Therapeutic Index in the United States for September 2003 to August 2004 (IMS Health) to obtain the USC and ATC classifications.

In addition, we focused on two further categories of NCEs of policy interest, i.e. biotech products and orphan products. We utilized the IMS database to identify the category of biological drugs. We defined an orphan product as an NCE launched in the United States within six months after FDA approval of its earliest orphan indication. This definition excludes NCEs that gained orphan indications after launch. The defined orphan products excluded those not yet available in the United States.

We then defined the corporation that first launched an NCE in the database and assigned its headquarters country as the nationality of the NCE. If more than one firm first launched an NCE, each firm received an equal share of that NCE for nationality assignment purposes. The IMS data base allows one to track the nationality of the company at the time of first global introduction, and therefore avoids issues raised by subsequent mergers that would change the corporation's identity.

A total of 919 NCEs were introduced from 1982 through 2003. Of these NCEs, 42 percent were global NCEs, 13 percent were first-in-class NCEs, 10 percent were biotech products, and 8 percent were orphan products. First-in-class NCEs, biotech products, and orphan products were more likely to be global products – 76 percent, 56 percent, and 61 percent, respectively.

Key Findings of the Grabowski and Wang Study

Two important results emerged from the Grabowski and Wang analysis. First, the observed trends suggest that the relative quality of NCEs has increased over time. In particular, the strong downward trend observed in total new chemical entities by many researchers is moderated when one looks at more selective measures of drug quality – namely trends in global drugs, first-in-class drugs, biotech and orphan products. This is shown in Figure 5-1, reproduced from the Grabowski and Wang study. In particular, all of these product categories have grown relative to total introductions over time. Furthermore, first-in-class, biotech, and orphan drugs have exhibited significant positive growth over time.

A second important finding relates to the source of quality-adjusted outputs across countries. Table 5-1 shows the nationality of NCEs from the Grabowski and Wang study based on the headquarters location of the company making the initial global introduction. European companies introduced the most NCEs in both periods as well as the most global NCEs. U.S. firms introduced the most first-in-class, biotech NCEs and orphan NCEs. U.S. leadership in these three categories was more pronounced in the 1993 to 2003 period, accounting for 48 percent of first-in-class drugs, 52 percent of biotech drugs, and 55 percent of orphan drugs.

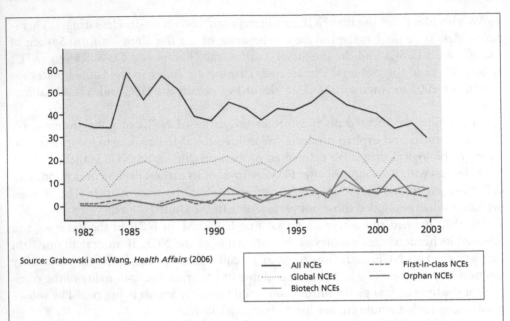

Source: Grabowski and Wang, *Health Affairs* (2006)

Legend:
— All NCEs
········ Global NCEs
— Biotech NCEs
---- First-in-class NCEs
— Orphan NCEs

Year	All NCEs	Global NCEs	First-in-class	Biotech	Orphan
1982	36	10	5	0	1
1983	34	17	4	0	1
1984	34	9	4	0	2
1985	59	17	5	2	2
1986	47	19	5	1	1
1987	57	15	5	0	1
1988	51	17	6	2	3
1989	39	18	4	2	1
1990	37	19	5	1	2
1991	45	21	5	7	2
1992	43	17	5	4	4
1993	38	18	2	1	4
1994	42	15	3	5	4
1995	41	20	6	6	3
1996	44	29	6	7	5
1997	50	27	5	3	4
1998	45	25	10	14	6
1999	41	21	6	7	5
2000	39	11	5	4	6
2001	33	20	6	13	5
2002	35	– –	7	4	4
2003	29	– –	6	7	3

Figure 5-1. Annual Introduction on new chemical Entities (NCEs), by category, 1982-2033.

Table 5-1. Nationality of NCEs Based on Headquarters Location

Country	All NCEs		Global NCEs		First-in-Class NCEs		Biotech NCEs		Orphan NCEs	
	82-92	93-03	82-92	93-03	82-92	93-03	82-92	93-03	82-92	93-03
Europe	230	183	99	112	23	27	6	23	9	20
Japan	125	88	12	12	5	3	5	9	1	0
USA	120	152	66	81	24	30	9	37	10	27
ROW	7	13	3	1	0	2	0	2	0	2
Total	482	437	179	206	53	62	19	71	20	49

Source: Grabowski and Wang, Health Affairs (2006).

Drug quality measures and the current analysis

In this paper, I extend the results of the Grabowski and Wang analysis by focusing on the country of discovery for the global, first-in-class, biotech and orphan categories using patent information. As a group, these categories should capture all the important therapeutic advances over this period. Before doing so, I discuss the rationale of each of the quality-adjusted indicators in this sector. Donald Light has questioned whether these categories capture scientific novelty and commercial significance rather than therapeutic benefits to patients[6]. In the rest of this section, I discuss the basis for using each of these measures as an indicator of various quality attributes of new drug introductions. I also make some marginal adjustments in the data sample, relative to our earlier paper.

First-in-class Drugs

First-in-class drug introductions provide physicians with novel mechanisms to treat patient illnesses and diseases. In terms of clinical benefits, a majority of the identified first-in-class drugs in our 1982-2003 sample were ranked as important therapeutic advances by the FDA[7]. Many firms pursue promising leads simultaneously and significant drug progress occurs both by the introduction of novel new classes and the evolution of products in these classes over time. In this competitive process, first-in-class drugs represent important milestones in the addition of new classes of medicines into the physician's arsenal. At the same time, subsequent introductions within a new therapeutic class can provide additional benefits to patients in terms of improved attributes or new indications[8]. While only one drug in a class can be the first approval, subsequent drug introductions that provide significant advances tend to diffuse rapidly across countries and become global or consensus drugs.

It is instructive to consider some of the important new drug classes that have occurred in the 1982-2003 period covered by our analysis. There has been a steady stream of novel drug categories. A more detailed list of these new classes and early entrants for the U.S. market is provided by DiMasi and colleagues[9].

The 1982-1992 sub-sample period saw the introduction of several new classes that addressed disease areas with few or inadequate treatments (e.g. the nucleoside reverse transcriptase inhibitors to treat HIV infections, the quinolones and the extended spectrum macrolides to treat bacterial infections, and various new classes such as taxanes to treat cancers). In addition, new classes were introduced that improved treatment effectiveness and patient tolerability for widespread medical problems such as depression, cholesterol reduction, migraine, and GERD (e.g. the SSRIs, statins, triptans and proton pump inhibitors).

Notable therapeutic advances in the 1993 to 2003 period included the introduction of protease inhibitors that were used in combination with nucleoside and non-nucleoside reverse transcriptase inhibitors for HIV infection. These antiretroviral combination protocols revolutionized the treatment of AIDS[10]. In addition, several new classes of cancer treatments were introduced that included the topoisemerase-I inhibitors for colorectal cancer, the tyrosine kinase inhibitors to treat leukemia, and the epidermal growth factor receptor kinase inhibitors for various types of cancer. Other new classes of drugs introduced during this period included the selective estrogen receptive modulators to treat osteoporosis, the angiotension-receptor blockers for hypertension, the glycoprotein IIb/III antagonists to treat acute myocardial infarction and unstable angina, and the carbonic anhydrase inhibitors to treat glaucoma.

In constructing the category of first-in-class drug introductions, G&W used a unique combination of the ATC and USC classification codes. This permitted a more representative grouping of new classes than utilizing either source individually. One limitation was the fact that both classification codes were only available for drugs approved and marketed in the United States. Given the size and significance of the U.S. market, there are strong economic incentives to introduce important new classes of drugs in the United States. However, some new classes of drugs introduced first in Europe or Japan may not have been available in the United States by 2003, especially if they were launched toward the end of our sample period. To check for the possibility of such omissions, I have examined additional information sources for the sample of drugs that are available in the United Kingdom or Japan since 1982, but were not available in the United States before 2003[11]. I also considered whether any drugs that qualify as first-in-class drugs under our criteria were available worldwide before 2003 and subsequently introduced into the United States from 2003 through October 2009. These supplementary searches yielded one additional first-in-class drug that was assigned to Europe based on the nationality of the firm discovering and introducing this product[12].

Biologics

The biotech industry is a relatively new source of medical innovation. The first wave of biotech products focused on recombinant forms of natural substances. The initial approvals were for synthetic human insulin in 1982 and human growth hormone in 1985. This was followed by a number of advances in the first decade of biotech products. Other notable biologicals during this first decade included erythropoietin, used extensively for dialysis patients and as supportive care for cancer and AIDS patients, filgrastim for neutropenia, and interferon alpha indicated for hepatitis C and leukemia.

The growing contribution of the biological sector is particularly evident in the 1993-2003 period. A newer class of biotech products focused on monoclonal antibodies and other types of proteins. These products were targeted to many life threatening diseases and illnesses with high unmet need. For example, the TNF inhibitors introduced in the late 1990s have approved indications for rheumatoid arthritis, psoriasis and Crohn's disease. Several of the new monoclonal antibody introductions in the oncology area have played a significant role in improving survival. These new products included the introduction of rituximab in 1997, trastuzumab in 1998, and bevacizumab in early 2004[13]. As discussed further below, these first-in-class and new biological products were disproportionately discovered in the United States, but often developed in collaboration with both U.S. and foreign headquartered companies.

Orphan Compounds

The number of orphan products also dramatically increased in the wake of the 1984 Orphan Drug Act in the United States. This law provided tax credits and market exclusivity incentives for products targeting rare diseases. Japan passed orphan drug legislation in 1993 and the European Union in 1999. Some of the notable orphan drug introductions since 1982 include therapies for multiple sclerosis, Gaucher's disease, and rare forms of cancer. Most of the new orphan drugs introduced in the United States are rated as important therapeutic advances by the FDA, and several qualify for the accelerated approval and fast track programs[14].

To address whether these are orphan products currently available in Europe and Japan but not in the United States, I examined all orphan products for the European Union and Japan, based on lists of approved orphan drugs for these countries. For these compounds, I first identified whether the product was a new molecular entity and also that the first-approved use was an orphan indication as in our earlier study for U.S. approvals. This yielded two additional orphan products assigned to Japanese firms and one additional orphan product assigned to an EU firm[15].

Global or Consensus Drugs

As discussed, global drug introductions drugs launched in a majority of the world's largest markets have been utilized by a number of past researchers as an indicator of a drug's commercial and therapeutic importance. This measure also can reflect marketing capacity and multinational structure of the originating organization compared to more selective measures such as first-in-class drugs. One limiting feature of our prior definition of global NCEs is that European countries make up four of the seven G7 countries that we used as the benchmark countries in our prior analysis. This gives European countries the greatest weight in the consensus measures. In particular, in our prior study, a drug could be considered global by diffusing only through the four largest markets of Europe. Although the United States and Japan constitute the two largest pharmaceutical markets, they receive only two "votes" while the much smaller European country markets receive four votes out of seven in measuring global introductions. When focusing on Europe as a single entity and drawing comparisons with the United States and Japan as in the current analysis, a more selective measure of global introductions is warranted.

In the analysis which follows, I define a global drug as one that must be marketed in six of the seven largest markets. This means that even for those drugs introduced in the four European countries, it must still be introduced in at least two of the other three G7 countries (United States, Japan and Canada) to be considered a global drug. Under this definition, there are 256 global drugs, or roughly 30% of the full sample of 919 worldwide introductions over the 1982 to 2003 sample period. This compares to 385 NCEs or roughly 40% of total introductions that diffuse through four or more of the G7 countries[16]. The more selective measure utilized here focuses on drugs representing consensus introductions that are approved in nearly all of the leading pharmaceutical country markets. This should also make the global measures in this analysis a more targeted index from the standpoint of a "must have" addition to the physicians' therapeutic arsenal in treating patients.

Total Sample of First-in-Class, Biotech, Global and Orphan Drugs

The combined sample of first-in-class, biotech and global introductions, has 380 introductions originating in the United States, Europe or Japan that qualify for one or more of these categories[17]. This is the sample of introductions for which I analyze the geographical area of discovery in the current analysis. This sample is also utilized to compare nationality based on the NCE inventor's region to those based on the introducing firm's headquarter location.

NCE inventor region versus firm headquarters region

Methodology and Data

To gain further insights on where a particular NCE was invented, I have assembled patent data on the sample of all first-in-class, biotech, global and orphan drug introductions. This data allows determining the inventors and affiliated organizations for each introduction, and correspondingly, the location of the R&D laboratory that originated the drug introduction. This measure is an interesting indicator of innovative performance in its own right, and also allows constructing alternative measures of R&D productivity to compare with those based on the nationality of firms making the first global introduction of an NCE.

As our first data source on patents, I utilize patent information from the United States and the United Kingdom. Both countries allow companies to restore part of the patent time lost in clinical development and regulatory review. The firm can only extend one patent, and this generally will be the core invention that offers the most protection (i.e. the composition of matter in the case of a new chemical entity). Where no patent information is available on a global introduction from these U.S. and UK patent files, I utilize the core patent listed in IMS R&D Focus, as well as information on the originator or innovation listed in the Pharma Projects, to determine who discovered the drug and the country of origin. I am able to determine inventors and country of origin for all but a small percentage of the total observations in the combined first-in-class, biotech, global and orphan drug samples. For a few cases where this information was missing, I utilize information available on the internet to establish the region of origin. These were generally attributed to foreign rather than U.S. companies[18].

The above approach allows me to identify for each drug introduction in the combined sample: (i) the country or region of discovery using patent data, and (ii) the location of the headquarters of the firm making the first global introduction using IMS New Product Focus database. When there are different companies involved in discovery and introduction, the country of discovery is assigned based on the location of the R&D lab that invented the compound. On the other hand, the headquarters location of the company making the first introduction generally provides information on where the compound's development was supported and carried forward to the point of worldwide introduction. Even when the same company is the discoverer and introducer, these two measures may be different when an R&D subsidiary located in a foreign location is the discoverer of a new compound. However, the "parent company" would still normally play a role in supporting the compound's development. In the current analysis, the region of discovery is the main focus of interest and the firm headquarters region provides a useful point of comparison.

Results

Figure 5-2 provides a summary of our findings regarding the 380 drug introductions that qualify either as first-in-class, biotech, global or orphan drug products for the full 1982 to 2003 period. Figure 5-2 shows that, based on NCE inventor region, the United States is the source of 52% of these worldwide introductions, Europe is the originator of 38%, and Japan accounts for 9%. When the classification is based on the firm headquarters region, the U.S. headquartered firms introduced 46% of these introductions compared to 45% for European firms and 9% for Japanese firms.

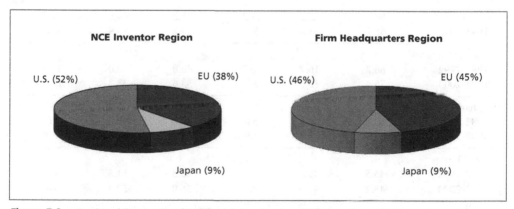

Figure 5-2.   Combined first-in-class, biotech, global and orphan NCE shares by region.

Table 5-2 provides disaggregated information for each category and subperiod. The percentage shares of the United States based on region of invention are larger than those based on firm headquarters' region for all four categories of novel introductions. For example, if one considers the United States, European and Japanese shares in discovering first-in-class drugs, the United States accounts for just over 50% of these introductions in the 1982-1992 period, increasing to 58.3% in the 1993-2003 period. This compares to invention shares by Europe in the mid 30% over these two periods and shares for Japan that are in the 5-10% range. Clearly, the United States has been the country of origin for these novel first-in-class new therapies, and the United States' prominence has been growing over time.

An even more dramatic picture emerges for biotech products in Table 5-2. In particular, for the 1993-2003 introductions, the United States was the country of origin in three quarters of the introductions. This compares to originating shares of 15.9% for Europe and 8.7% for Japan during this period. My analysis for this category is confirmed in a recent OECD study that examined the country where original development occurred for 138 approved biotherapies introduced between January 1989 and January 2000. The OECD data indicates that U.S. located labs accounted for the initial development of 73.5% of biotherapies, compared to 18.1% for Europe and 8.4% for Japan[19]. These values are very similar to the ones we obtained using patent information to determine geographical region of discovery for the period 1993-2003 in Table 5-2.

In terms of the third category of drug introductions in Table 5-2, orphan compounds, a similar pattern is also observed. When orphan drug introductions are classified by geographical region of origin, the United States accounted for over 60% of the orphan drugs in the 1993-2003 period compared to Europe's 33.3% and Japan's 39%. Most of the orphan drugs are concentrated in this period. This strong U.S. leadership

Table 5-2. Shares in First-in-Class, Biotech, Global and Orphan NCEs by Region 1982-1992 and 1993-2003

Type of NCE	NCE Inventor Region (%)			Firm Headquarters Region (%)		
	U.S.	EU	Japan	U.S.	EU	Japan
First-in-Class						
1982-1992	50.9	37.7	11.3	46.2	44.2	9.6
1993-2003	56.7	38.3	5.0	49.2	45.9	4.9
Biotech Drugs						
1982-1992	66.7	16.7	16.7	45.0	30.0	25.0
1993-2003	75.4	15.9	8.7	53.6	33.3	13.0
Orphan Drugs						
1982-1992	55.0	40.0	5.0	50.0	45.0	5.0
1993-2003	62.9	33.3	3.9	54.0	42.0	4.0
Global Drugs						
1982-1992	43.5	49.6	7.0	43.5	51.8	4.6
1993-2003	48.2	41.9	9.9	36.9	57.3	5.8

Source: Author's own analysis.

is reflective of U.S. policy initiatives in this area. It was not only the first country to pass legislation on orphan drugs, but has more generous tax credits and other incentives[20].

In the case of global drugs, Europe was the source of discovery for more of these drugs in the 1982-1992 period than the United States (49.6% to 43.5%). However, this pattern reversed in the 1993-2003 period in which the United States discovered more global drugs than Europe (48.2% to 41.9%). Interestingly, firms headquartered in Europe were the first introducers of the most global products in both periods. In the 1993-2003 period, for example, European headquartered firms introduced 57.3% of all global drugs even though only 41.9% were discovered in Europe. By contrast, the United States headquartered firms introduced 36.9% of these global drugs, but the U.S. geographical area accounted for 48.9% of discoveries in this period.

As noted, the shares based on the headquarters location of the introducing company are best interpreted as indicators of development support in those cases when discovery and development takes place in different organizations or locations. Viewed in this way, U.S. firms also emerge as leading developers and introducers of novel new products, but the differences are not nearly as great as those based on the geographical region of discovery. The difference between U.S. and European firms in developing first-in-class drugs is only a few percentage points, whereas European firms lead in developing global drugs (but not in the area of discovery as discussed above). The U.S. headquartered firm leadership is most pronounced as first introducers of biotech and orphan drugs.

These patterns are consistent with several trends described in the industry trade literature. In particular, many European firms focused increased R&D in the United States, both in their own labs and in partnership with U.S. development stage firms. This is reflected in the differences between output measures based on location of discovery versus headquarters of first introducer. For example, for the 17.5 global drugs first introduced by Hoffman LaRoche, only 6 were discovered in Europe whereas 9.5 originated in the United States and 2 originated in Japan. Some of these U.S. discovered drugs originated in its U.S. partner, Genentech, while others were discovered in their U.S. laboratories in New Jersey and California[21]. As another example, Glaxo-Wellcome became the industry leader in new product introductions indicated for AIDS based on research programs in anti-viral drugs located in the United States[22]. However, all these introductions would be assigned to Europe in classifications based on the location of their European headquarters.

Our results on the importance of the United States as the country of origin for new pharmaceuticals and biotherapies are also confirmed for a much broader class of inventions. Gambardella and colleagues examined the location of inventions for all European patents filed between 1978 and 1997. For the most recent decade covered in their work, 1988-1997, the United States originated a larger share of European patents in both pharmaceuticals and biotherapies than those that originated in all the European countries, and U.S. shares were growing over time. The same report provides an analysis of licensing agreements in R&D, which shows the United States as the primary source of licensing agreements in Europe with shares exceeding those of Europe and Japan from the three regions of U.S., Europe, and Japan[23].

R&D Productivity by region

In a follow-on article to G&W's study in *Health Affairs* in 2009, Donald Light utilized our data on international drug introductions to offer a different perspective on innovative performance across national industries[24]. In particular, he focuses on R&D productivity by European, U.S., and Japanese firms. He claims that in terms of new drugs introductions per R&D dollar invested, the European industry is ahead of its U.S. counterparts. However, his analysis is subject to a number of conceptual, as well as empirical, issues.

Conceptual and Measurement Problems

Light's R&D productivity measure for the United States, Europe and Japan confounds two different concepts of nationality. His numerator is based on a company's nationality: the number of new drugs accounted for by companies headquartered in a particular country or region. His denominator is area-specific: the R&D performed in a particular country or region by all the domestic and foreign companies operating in that geographical area. If European headquartered companies obtain a higher percentage of introductions from discoveries that originated in the U.S. compared to what U.S. headquartered companies obtain from Europe, Light's method would result in underestimation of R&D productivity in the United States, relative to Europe. Our findings from patent data indicate this is the case.

If one considers the number of drugs discovered or developed in a region divided by appropriately lagged R&D inputs, one would obtain a more consistent means of R&D productivity than Light's measure, which mixes different national concepts. At best, however, R&D productivity measures by nationality can be suggestive and not determinative because there are no data series available that precisely match the values in the numerator with the denominator. All measures are necessarily qualified by the fact that some of the relevant R&D expenditure will not be included in existing industry data (e.g. R&D funded by private equity sources). Furthermore, R&D development often spans multiple countries and it is not possible with existing data to parse out the amounts expended in each country over the R&D life cycle for particular introductions. Given these qualifications, it is still instructive to consider how robust Light's results are to alternative, more plausible formulations of R&D productivity.

R&D Funding Patterns by Region

A second problem associated with Light's R&D productivity analysis is that he uses an inappropriate lag structure for R&D expenditures. In particular, Light divides the 1982-1992 introductions for each national region by R&D expenditures undertaken in the year 1990. Correspondingly, he divides 1993 to 2003 period introductions by R&D expenditures undertaken in 2000.

A central finding of numerous R&D studies is that a lengthy R&D process in pharmaceuticals generally spans a decade or more. In particular, DiMasi et al. observe a twelve-year period from synthesis to approval for the average new drug approval in the United States[25]. Moreover, more than half of the out-of-pocket R&D expenditures (including failures) undertaken to discover and develop a new drug are made by year six of this process. Given these facts, the R&D period for 1982 to 1992 introductions would typically cover 1971-1991 with a median year of 1981. Similarly, the R&D process for 1993 to 2003 introductions spans the 1982 to 2002 period with a median year of 1992.

Using R&D expenditures at the end of each period is not only inappropriate given the lengthy R&D process in pharmaceuticals, but it also introduces further problems associated with exchange rate fluctuations. In particular, U.S. exchange rates against the euro were uncharacteristically high in 2000. In Light's analysis, the exchange rate was 1.27 dollars to a Euro in 1990, compared to 0.92 dollars to a euro in 2000[26]. Exchange rate differences between 1990 and 2000 account for approximately one-half of the increased share of R&D expenditures for the United States during the periods in Light's calculations. Therefore, U.S. productivity values are correspondingly lowered in Light's analysis of the 1993-2003 period as a result of these exchange rate fluctuations.

Using information from the R&D cost studies to construct an appropriate lag structure, I employ a three-year period on regional R&D shares centered around 1981 for the 1982-1992 introductions, and centered around 1992 for the 1993-2003 set of introductions[27]. Selecting these years for the lag between R&D and NCEs also effectively moderates the exchange rate fluctuations that beset Light's analysis. In particular, the exchange rates for these two periods are roughly comparable and more characteristic of the overall period encompassed by the complete R&D series[28].

Figure 5-3 shows the percentage breakdown of R&D expenditures for the United States, Europe and Japan for the relevant periods. Europe accounted for the highest R&D shares in both of the periods. Its share is 50.9% in the 1980-1982 period, and 44.8% in the 1991-1993 period[29]. Correspondingly, the United States experienced a modest increase in its R&D shares over the two periods (33.1% to 35.7%) as did Japan (16.1% to 19.5%). In contrast, Light's analysis has the United States' share increasing from 33.3%

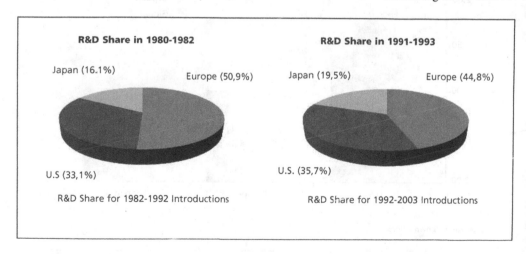

R&D Share in 1980-1982

Japan (16.1%)   Europe (50,9%)

U.S (33,1%)

R&D Share for 1982-1992 Introductions

R&D Share in 1991-1993

Japan (19,5%)   Europe (44,8%)

U.S. (35,7%)

R&D Share for 1992-2003 Introductions

Figure 5-3. R&D Shares in 1980-1982 and 1991-1993. *Source: Author's own analysis.*

in 1990 to 47.8% in 2000. However, as noted, in using these years to calculate R&D shares for his productivity analysis, he fails to account properly for the long lags between R&D inputs and outputs, and R&D shares are also heavily influenced by the very strong U.S. dollar in 2000.

Proportionality Ratios

One can express a region's R&D productivity measure as a proportionality ratio. In particular, under this approach the shares in the output measures for the United States, Europe and Japan are divided by the corresponding R&D shares for each sub-period. A proportionality ratio above one implies a region's output share exceeds its R&D share, a relative measure of that region's innovative performance.

Figure 5-4 shows the proportionality ratios for the 1993-2003 period. These are obtained by dividing the share of discoveries for the different introduction categories accounted for by the United States, Europe and Japan (from Table 5-2) by the lagged R&D funding shares (from Figure 5-4). As this figure shows, the United States had proportionality ratios in excess of 1.0 in each category (ranging from 1.35 to 2.11), whereas Europe had ratios below one (0.36 to 0.94), and Japan had the worst performance for these novel drug categories (ranging from 0.20 to 0.51). This pattern is generally repeated across all these four classes for the 1982-1992 period. These are shown in Table 5-3.

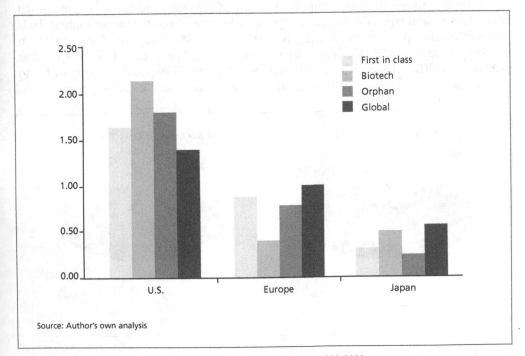

Source: Author's own analysis

Figure 5-4. Proportionality Ratios Based on NCE Inventor Region 1993-2003.

Indeed, the proportionality ratios for the United States based on region of discovery increased between the first and second period for all four categories of drug introductions, and are always substantially greater than 1.0 in value, whereas those for Europe and Japan are much smaller in value.

Table 5-3 also indicates that even if one uses an output measure based on headquarters location of the region first introducing a new product, the United States has proportionality ratios above 1.0. By contrast, Europe's ratios are generally smaller and below 1.0 in value. The only exception is for global drugs, where Europe's ratio increased sharply in 1993-2003 in accord with the trend toward greater licensing activity from —and R&D investment in— the United States, as discussed earlier.

The proportionality ratios based on company headquarters location give a different view of nationality. They are more selective indications of drug development support and ownership than drug discovery. In any case, they contradict Light's findings. He concludes that Europe's productivity exceeded that of the U.S. in first-in-class and global drugs in 1992-3003, and that they were catching up to the United States in biotech and orphan compounds. This conclusion, however, was based on an implausible lag structure between R&D and introductions. When a more appropriate lag structure is utilized to compute these measures, the finding that Europe has greater and increasing research productivity in these innovative new drug categories is not supported by the data[30].

As previously noted, all R&D productivity analyses must be qualified by the fact that currently available data does not permit establishing exact matches between outputs in the numerator and the appropriate R&D expenditures in the denominator for particular geographic regions. Nevertheless, after making reasonable corrections to Light's productivity analysis, I conclude that his findings are not robust. They do not support his

Table 5-3. Proportionality Ratios Based on NCE Inventor Region and Firm Headquarters Region 1982-1992 and 1993-2003

Type of NCE	NCE Inventor Region (%)			Firm Headquarters Region (%)		
	U.S.	EU	Japan	U.S.	EU	Japan
First-in-Class						
1982-1992	1.54	0.74	0.71	1.40	0.87	0.60
1993-2003	1.59	0.86	0.26	1.38	1.02	0.25
Biotech Drugs						
1982-1992	2.02	0.33	1.03	1.36	0.59	1.55
1993-2003	2.11	0.36	0.45	1.50	0.74	0.67
Orphan Drugs						
1982-1992	1.66	0.79	0.31	1.51	0.88	0.31
1993-2003	1.76	0.74	0.20	1.51	0.94	0.21
Global Drugs						
1982-1992	1.31	0.97	0.43	1.31	1.02	0.29
1993-2003	1.35	0.94	0.51	1.03	1.28	0.30

Source: Author's own analysis.

conclusion that Europe has experienced greater productivity with respect to the quality-oriented NCEs categories.

Conclusions and policy considerations

One of the key new findings of the current analysis is that when new drugs groups, such as first-in-class, biotech, global, and orphan drug products, are collected by country of discovery using data on patented inventions, the United States is the world leader in discovering these innovative compounds. There is net outflow of inventive activity from U.S. R&D laboratories to the rest of the world. This finding is consistent with other recent international comparative analyses sponsored by the OECD and the European Union[31].

The leadership of the United States in the innovative process, which has grown over time, is reflective of both supply and demand side developments. Since the early 1980s, U.S. industrial policy has fostered many new discovery-oriented firms in the life sciences through public support of basic biomedical research, favorable university technology transfer processes, and highly supportive private and public equity markets. While U.S. institutions promoting these life science entities have been more developed than abroad, other countries are closing the gap, as has been noted in earlier papers[32].

On the demand side, the shift toward more innovative introductions in the United States has been fostered by the growth of managed care plans and pharmacy benefit management firms. These plans utilize various instruments —including tiered formularies with differential co-payments, prior authorization, and step therapy— to manage drug benefits. Innovative products with few close substitutes can earn premium prices, but drugs with close substitutes or generic alternatives are subject to strong price competition. Prices in foreign countries are subject to competitive pressure through reference pricing and other approaches, but innovative products generally obtain lower prices than in the United States. Often, new products receive little more than much older products with similar indications but fewer therapeutic benefits[33].

Many studies point out that price controls in particular countries have encouraged imitative type introductions because they under-reward innovation relative to imitation. In addition, countries will often offer more favorable pricing decisions to companies that invest domestically in terms of facilities and R&D. Favoritism or protection of the domestic industry nurtures a more imitative industry. Historically, Japan, France, and Italy have provided prominent examples[34]. Some firms eventually look beyond the domestic market and produce innovative products that take advantage of global opportunities, but many retain an imitative focus because of price regulation and protectionism. This helps to explain how patterns of poor performance across national industries can persist over time and erode only slowly, even in a globally-oriented industry like pharmaceuticals.

Some observers such as Donald Light imply that price controls in the U.S. market, as practiced widely throughout Europe, would not affect the availability of useful new drug introductions produced globally. His R&D productivity measures are flawed empirically and conceptually, and do not provide support for this position. More importantly, numerous studies indicate that if one lowers the rewards for innovation significantly in the world's largest market, R&D expenditures will be affected[35]. This will be true not only for U.S. firms but for foreign firms that plan to market their drugs here. The R&D process is long, costly, and uncertain, and a cut in R&D expenditures will affect both the quality and quantity of new drug introductions on a global basis. Start-up firms and development R&D companies with early stage risky R&D projects are likely to be most adversely affected by such price controls. These firms have been disproportionately located in the United States. Light's advocacy of greater use of comparative effectiveness and cost-benefit analyses is a worthy goal, but there is more to be gained from implementation in a market-based system, insulated from political considerations and bureaucratic implementation.

Public policy toward biopharmaceutical innovation has many interacting parts, including support of basic research and technology transfers, intellectual property protection provisions, regulation of product safety and efficacy, and pricing reimbursement of approved medicines[36]. No country has a claim to optimal policies in all these dimensions, and these policies are subject to considerable legislative and regulatory changes over time. The U.S. ban on federally supported stem cell research is an example of how policy actions can adversely affect a region's innovative performance and location of new drug discoveries[37]. Nevertheless, our analysis on where novel new drug discoveries have originated since the early 1980s indicates that, on balance, the United States has maintained the most positive environment to stimulate biopharmaceutical innovation.

REFERENCES

1. H. Grabowski and Y.R. Wang, "The Quantity and Quality of Worldwide New Drug Introductions, 1982-2003", *Health Affairs* 25(2), (2006): 452-460
2. P. Danzon, S. Nicholson, and N.S. Periera, "Productivity in pharmaceutical-biotechnology R&D: The role of experience and alliances", *Journal of Health Economics* 24 No. 2 (2005): 317-339; A. Arora, A. Fosfuri and A. Gambardella, *Markets for Technology: The economics of innovation and corporate strategy* (Cambridge, MA: MIT Press, 2001).
3. D.W. Light, "Global Drug Discovery: Europe is Ahead", *Health Affairs* 28(5) (2009): W969-977.
4. National Academy of Engineering, *The Competitive Status of the U.S. Pharmaceutical Industry*, Washington, DC: National Academy Press, 1983.
5. H. Grabowski, "An Analysis of U.S. International Competitiveness in Pharmaceuticals", *Managerial and Decision Economics* 10(1), 1989: 27-33; L.G. Thomas, "Implicit Industrial Policy: The Triumph of Britain and the Failure of France in Global Pharmaceuticals", *Industrial and Corporate Change* 3(2), 1984:451-489; L. G. Thomas, III, *The Japanese Pharmaceutical Industry*, Cheltenham, U.K.: Edgar Elgar, 2001.
6. Light, "Global Drug Discovery", op. cit.
7. In particular, 57% of the first-in-class drugs were ranked as important advances. This compares to 40% of all NCEs being ranked as important therapeutic advances. H. Grabowski and Y. Richard Wang, "The Quantity and Quality of Worldwide New Drug Introductions 1992 2003", *Health Affairs*, vol. 25 no. 2 (2006), p. 459.
8. E.R. Berndt, I.M. Cockburn and K.A. Grenpin, "The Impact of Incremental Innovation in Biopharmaceuticals", *PharmcoEconomics* 22 Supp. 4 (2006): 69-86.
9. Research by DiMasi and colleagues indicates that the time between the first entrant in a new class and the second-in-class products, has steadily declined over time, so that new treatment approaches typically involve a rapid introduction of alternative therapies within a class. J.A. DiMasi and C. Paquette, "The Economics of Follow-on Drug Research and Development: Trends in Entry Rates and Timing of Development", *PharmcoEconomics* 22 Supp. 2 (2004): 1-14. J.A.

DiMasi and L.B. Faden, "Follow-on Drug R&D: New Data on Trends in Entry Rates and the Timing of Development", Tufts University Center for the Study of Drug Development, unpublished manuscript, 2009.

10. Since the 1990s, the U.S. death rates from AIDS dropped about 70% after the advent of new treatment regimes. See, for example, CASCADE Collection "Determinants of Survival Following HIV-1 seroconversion after Introduction of HAART", *The Lancet* vol. 362, (2003); pp. 1267-1274.

11. In particular, we started with the ATC codes for all these drugs available outside the United States to see whether these drugs received a new class code. This is available on the WHO Collaborating Centre for Drug Statistics Methodology (http://www.whocc.no/), and we also used complementary internet data sources and the USC codes for any of these drugs that became available in the United States after 2003.

12. This product was telithromycin (Ketek), a member of the ketolide class which was first introduced worldwide in October 2001 and subsequently in the United States in April 2004.

13. Bevacizumab (Avastin) was first approved in February 2004 just after the December 2003 sample period of our analysis. For a description of the lengthy development process of bevacizumab, which was first isolated in 1989 by scientists at Genentech, see H. Grabowski, "Follow-on biologics: data exclusivity and the balance between innovation and competition", *Nature Reviews Drug Discovery*, vol. 7 no. 6 (June, 2008), pp. 479-488.

14. http://www.fda.gov/ForIndustry/DevelopingProductsforRareDiseasesConditions/default.htm Tufts Center for the Study of Drug Development, "FDA's Fast Track Program Results in 62% Approval Rate after First 3 Years", Impact Report, 3, No. 1 (Jan/Feb 2001).

15. We obtained a list of approved orphan drugs introduced in Japan since the passage of the legislation in 1993 from Pacific Bridge Medical. For information on this publication, "Orphan Drugs in Asia 2009", see their website, http://www.pacificbridgemedical.com/. A list of orphan designated authorized medicines in Europe is available from the EMEA website http://www.emea.europa.eu/ pdfs/human/comp/56357508en.pdf. The two additional orphan drugs assigned to Japan were mecasermin in 1994 and taltirelin in 2000, and the one for Europe was migulast in 2003.

16. H. Grabowski and Y. Richard Wang, "The Quantity and Quality of Worldwide New Drug Introductions 1992-2003", *Health Affairs*, vol. 25 no. 2 (2006), p. 455.

17. In addition, there were five introductions originating outside of the United States, Europe or Japan in at least one of these four categories that are not included, as I am focusing on the three regions that dominate pharmaceutical R&D innovation.

18. After utilizing all the available information from the patent data registries and IMS and Pharma Projects databases on country of discovery, we obtained information on the innovator for six introductions from other internet sources. In these cases where inventors were located in more than one geographical region, we selected the region where the majority of the inventors were located.

19. OECD Biotechnology Statistics 2009 (http://www.oecd.org/dataoecd/4/23/42833898.pdf), p. 85. This analysis utilized Pharma Projects database of drugs to determine the geographical location of initial development.

20. For discussion of the differences in orphan drug laws for the United States, Japan and Europe, see H. Kettler, "Narrowing the Gap between Provision and Need for Medicines in Developing Countries" (London: Office of Health Economics, 2000) 40-43.

21. Examples of biotech products discovered by the U.S. partner, Genentech, and introduced worldwide by Roche include rituximab and trastuzumab. Products emerging from its U.S. R&D laboratories in Nutley, NJ and Palo Alto, CA included valganciclovir and mycophenolate mofetil.

22. R. Landau, B. Achiladelis and A. Scriabine, *Pharmaceutical Innovation: Revolutionizing human health* (Philadelphia, PA: Chemical Heritage Foundation, 1999) p. 352-356; Dr. Gertrude Elion and George Hitchings, who worked in the Research Triangle Park labs of Burroughs Wellcome in North Carolina, shared the 1988 Nobel Prize for Medicine with Sir James Black for "important principles of drug development". According to the Nobel Committee, their research was instrumental in creating several important new drugs, including anti-viral drugs for herpes and AIDS. Burroughs and Wellcome, in conjunction with the NIH, developed the first drug for AIDS, Zidovudine (AZT). This drug was first synthesized as an anti-cancer drug n the 1060s by scientists

at Wayne State University, but proved ineffective in this use. Based on the discovery of AZT as an AIDS treatment, scientists in the anti-viral group at Burroughs Wellcome were awarded a method of U.S. patent in 1985 by the U.S. Patent Office. Judy Forman, "3 Share Nobel Price for Medicine", *Boston Globe*, Tuesday, October 18, 2008, p. 1; H. Grabowski, "Are the Economics of Pharmaceutical R&D Changing? Productivity, Patents and Political Pressures", *PharmacoEconomics* 22, suppl. 2 (2004); 15-24.

23   A. Gambardella, L. Orsenigo and F. Pammoli. "Global Competitiveness in Pharmaceuticals: A European Perspective", (Luxembourg: Officer for Official Publication of the European Communities, 2001) pg. 31, 51. For 1988-1997, the United States was the country of discovery for 44.9% of European pharmaceutical patents and 46.8% of the biotech patents versus 39.8% and 34.2% respectively emanating from European countries (Table 16, p. 38).

24. Light, "Global Drug Discovery", op. cit.

25. J. DiMasi, R. Hansen and H. Grabowski, "The Price of Innovation: New Estimates of Drug Development Costs", *Journal of Health Economics* 22(2) (2003): 151-185.

26. Federal Reserve's Statistical Rates http://www.federalreserve.gov/releases/h10/hist/default.htm

27. Data series on annual R&D expenditures assembled by the EFPIA, the European Federation of Pharmaceutical Industries and Associations beginning in 1980 are available in PAREXEL'S Bio/Pharmaceutical R&D Statistical Sourcebook 2007/2008, p. 283. Information on R&D expenditures in the United States is available from PhRMA Annual Survey 2007 (Washington, DC: Pharmaceutical Research and Manufacturers of America: 2007). It is also available in PAREXELS Sourcebook on page 4. Information on R&D expenditures in Japan is available from the Japan Pharmaceutical Manufacturers' Association (JPMA) Data Books, various annual editions.

28. Annual exchange rates for U.S. dollar to Euro in 1980-1982 ranged from 0.98 to 1.39 with a three-year average of 1.16. This compares to a range in annual exchange of 1.17 to 1.30 in 1991-1993 with a three-year average of 1.23.

29. To check on our approach, we also construct a variable lag model structure for 1993-2003 introductions using all of the R&D expenditure data by origin from the 1982-2002 years. This approach combines the appropriate weights derived from the DiMasi cost study for this 11-year span of introductions, together with the annual exchange rates for the 1982 to 2002 period. The R&D shares are not materially affected for 1993-2003 introductions whether one employs the three-year average around 1992, or alternatively uses a variable lag structure spanning the full 1981 to 2002 period. In particular, for 1993 to 2003 introductions, the weighted variable lag model yields shares of 44.4% for Europe, 37.3% for the United States, and 18.3% for Japan.

30. I have also analyzed proportionality ratios on all 919 introductions based on the headquarters country's count of introductions in the numerator. These data indicate that U.S., European and Japanese headquartered firms had shares of all drug introductions roughly proportional to the total R&D investment performed by all firms in their home regions during the 1993-2003 period. I have not undertaken an analysis based on the region of discovery for all 919 worldwide introductions using the patent databases. This would be an ambitious undertaking, given that many of these drugs were introduced in only one or two countries and patent databases are likely to be incomplete, especially when considering worldwide introductions from earlier periods. However, there is reason to expect that when regions are analyzed by NCE inventor location, the pattern observed in Exhibit 1 for the combined innovative drug categories would hold for larger samples. This notion is supported by the findings discussed earlier from a large universe of European patent data and licensing agreements.

31. A. Gambardella et al., "Global Competitiveness", p. 20, 31.

32. H. Grabowski and Y. Richard Wang, "The Quantity and Quality of Worldwide New Drug Introductions 1992-2003", *Health Affairs*, vol. 25 no. 2 (2006), pp. 458-459; F. M. Scherer, *New Prospectives on Economic Growth and Technological Innovation* (Washington: Brookings Institution, 1999).

33. P. Danzon and L. Chao, "Does Regulation Drive Out Competition in the Pharmaceutical Market?" *Journal of Law and Economics*, 49 No. 2 (2000): 311-357; P. Danzon, *Pharmaceutical Price Regulation: National Policies Versus Global Interests* (Washington: AEI 1997).

34. L.G. Thomas, *The Japanese Pharmaceutical Industry* (Chetenham, England: Edgar Elgar, 2001);

L.G. Thomas, "Implicit Industrial Policy: The Triumph of Britain and the Failure of France in Global Pharmaceuticals", *Industrial and Corporate Change* 3, No. 2. (1994): 451-489.

35.   F.M. Scherer, "The Link Between Gross Profitability and Pharmaceutical R&D Spending", *Health Affairs*, 20, No. 5 (2001): 216-220; C. Giaccotto, R.E. Santerre and J.A. Vernon, "Drug Prices and R&D Investment Behavior in the Pharmaceutical Industry", *Journal of Law and Economics* 48 No. 1 (2005); 194-214.

36.   F.M. Scherer, "U.S. Industrial Policy" in Adrian Towse, editor, *Industrial Policy and the Pharmaceutical Industry*, (London: Office of Health Economics, 1995).

37.   H. Grabowski. "Are the Economics of Pharmaceutical R&D Changing? Productivity, Patents and Political Pressures", *PharmcoEconomics* 22, suppl. 2 (2004): 15-24.

CHAPTER 6

The use of pay-for-performance for drugs: can it improve incentives for innovation?

Adrian Towse, Louis Garrison, and Ruth Puig-Peiró

Introduction

There has been a growth in interest in schemes that involve "paying for pills by results" (Pollock, 2007) i.e. "paying for performance" rather than merely "paying for pills". Hard-pressed health care payers want to know that they are getting what they are paying for - health and other benefits for patients. Pharmaceutical companies are not prepared to accept prices that they think do not reflect the innovative value that their expensive R&D investments are bringing to patients, the health care system and the broader economy. Paying for outcomes delivered is a way of "squaring the circle". Payers know they are getting value. Companies get a return that incentivises future innovation.

Yet this approach is highly controversial and is disliked by many health care providers, policymakers, and pharmaceutical companies. One scheme in particular, the UK National Health Service (NHS) Multiple Sclerosis (MS) Risk Sharing Scheme (RSS), has attracted fierce criticism (McCabe et al. 2010; Raftery, 2010). In this paper we:

- Define what we mean by pay-for-performance and the related terms used in discussions about these schemes;
- Set out a framework for understanding and interpreting these schemes;
- Explore with examples the types and numbers of schemes that exist;
- Discuss the benefits and weaknesses;
- Consider their value as an incentive for innovation.

In doing so we draw upon papers one or more of us has co-authored (Towse and Garrison, 2010; Carlson et al., 2010; Puig-Peiro et al. 2011).

What do we mean by pay-for-performance?

We use the term pay-for-performance to refer to an agreement between a payer and a pharmaceutical manufacturer where the price level and/or revenue received is related to the *future* performance of the product in either a research or real-world environment. This is broadly comparable to de Pouvourville's (2006) definition of "risk-sharing" as "a contract between two parties who agree to engage in a transaction in which (…) one party has sufficient confidence in its claims (…) that it is ready to accept a reward or a penalty depending on the observed performance". We therefore regard the terms as interchangeable and in this paper we use the term pay-for-performance.

Other terms used in this context include "conditional reimbursement", "coverage with evidence development" (CED) and "access with evidence development". We regard these terms as interchangeable and use CED. The implication is that some information is going to be collected and a review of reimbursement status is to be held at some later point. However, these arrangements may not specify either (i) what type of evidence is to be collected or (ii) how price/revenue and/or use is to be changed depending on what the evidence says about the product. There may only be an agreement, understanding, or requirement that some sort of review will take place after a certain period of time. We can therefore consider a pay-for-performance agreement a subset of CED arrangements where (i) and (ii) above *are* specified in advance. The others can perhaps best be summarized as "CED with renegotiation".

The term "only in research" (OIR) is sometimes also used, usually to indicate that there is not enough evidence to approve for CED. This contrasts with CED which can best be thought of as "only *with* research". The difference is that in the first case all patients must be included in the research if they are to be eligible for treatment. In the other case, it is only necessary that the research is conducted, not that all patients are part of it. Only in research is therefore best thought of as a "no". It typically involves restricting access to a small subgroup of the eligible population through recruitment to a Randomised Controlled Trial (RCT). Of course it could in theory involve full access to the technology for all patients subject to some data being collected on them (e.g. via inclusion in a patient registry). In this case it is, effectively, a form of CED. An example of this was the US Center for Medicare and Medicaid Services (CMS) coverage of implantable cardioverter defibrillators[i] where all patients were required to enrol in a registry[ii].

We also use the terms risk and uncertainty interchangeably. A distinction is sometimes made between them according to whether or not the *probabilities* of outcomes are known or not. This is not helpful in this context. Decision makers have to make assumptions. The role of evidence and analysis is to make them better informed. We therefore use the term uncertainty to refer to the extent to which the decision maker is unclear

---

[i] This scheme was controversial because key data were not collected and there was also no funding to analyse the data in order to revisit the coverage decision with more evidence.

[ii] Strictly, one could think of pay-for-performance agreements where each patient is required to be tracked, for example in a responder scheme, as a form of "only in research", but this would be unhelpful. Responder-type pay-for-performance schemes are best understood as a form of CED in which it is clear (i) what type of evidence is to be collected and (ii) how price/revenue is to be changed depending on what the evidence says.

whether or not they are making the right decision, i.e. the one they would make with perfect information about all aspects of the incremental impact of the drug.

Some jurisdictions use terms that are specific to their systems. For example, the UK has "flexible pricing" (FP) and "Patient Access Schemes" (PASs). Both are defined by the Pharmaceutical Price Regulation Scheme (PPRS) of 2009. Under flexible pricing, companies can apply to increase their price if the evidence supports it. It is agreed that NICE will use its normal evidence standards and the cost-effectiveness threshold it used earlier when initially agreeing to use the drug (Towse, 2010). However, no more detailed arrangements are outlined, and there are no requirements for resubmission. By contrast, PASs are agreement-specific. However, most are "financial" arrangements intended to provide the UK NHS with effective discounts from list price rather than being linked to "outcomes". The UK PASs therefore include pay-for-performance agreements but are mainly types of discount agreements[iii].

Italy has Managed Entry Agreements with a 2-year review point. In some cases these are financially oriented, taking the form of a maximum volume agreement, or a budget cap. In other cases they are intended to target treatments to responders. The Italian Medicines Agency (AIFA) uses the terms "cost sharing" (where there is a price reduction for initial treatment cycles until it is clear whether a patient is responding), "payment by results" (where the manufacturer reimburses the payer for non-responders) and "risk sharing" (where only 50% of the costs of the non-responders are reimbursed by the manufacturer). All are pay-for-performance agreements according to our criteria.

We can thus see pay-for-performance as an arrangement that is becoming of increasing interest to payers. We now consider whether it is an efficient way to reward and incentivise innovation.

A framework for understanding and interpreting pay-for-performance schemes

Towse and Garrison (2010) argue that "value of information" and "real option" theory offer the best framework for understanding and interpreting pay-for-performance schemes. Following Eckermann and Willan (2007) they state that payers have three decision choices with regard to a new drug: they can agree to list it for some or all of its licensed indications on the basis of current evidence without requiring additional research; they can refuse to list it (leaving manufacturers with the option of coming back with more evidence and/or a lower price); or they can list it subject to submission of additional evidence (in essence a "yes but"). Pay-for-performance can be seen as analogous to a form of "money back guarantee" for a consumer product. In the event of the product failing to perform, the buyer can get some or all of their money back. Indeed, Cook at al. (2008) have likened risk sharing agreements for drugs to a warranty. The payer has the right to sell the product back to the manufacturer. This is called a "put option". It is termed a "real option" because it relates to a physical product rather

---

[iii] An effective price discount, of course, also has an impact on uncertainty. It does not increase the payers' knowledge of the expected outcome but, for any given expected outcome and willingness to pay threshold, it does reduce the likelihood that the decision to adopt will subsequently turn out to have been wrong.

than a "financial option". Offering a put option alongside the product makes it more likely that the payer will say "yes but" rather than "no". The value of the option to the payer depends on the information that will be generated during the period it can be exercised. If no more information is generated the value may be zero – the payer has no better idea as to whether, on balance, the drug is likely to be value for money than when they adopted it.

Which one of the three decision choices the payer should make depends on the expected outcome (on the basis of current evidence) and the costs and benefits of additional evidence collection, which will reduce the uncertainty about underlying cost-effectiveness. "Value of information" calculations can be used to inform judgements about expected outcomes, the extent of uncertainty around these outcomes, and the likely benefits of collecting extra evidence. If there is substantial uncertainty as to the likely cost-effectiveness of a new drug in practice, it may make sense not to start using the drug but to collect additional information to reduce that uncertainty. Uncertainty has a cost for payers because it means there is a chance the drug does not represent value and so they will be wasting money and failing to spend the money on other health interventions that provide benefit to patients. Where there are also costs associated with reversing a decision to use a drug (it may even be impossible to change prescriber behaviour unless, in the extreme, the drug is found to be unsafe and withdrawn from the market) then getting the initial decision right becomes all the more important for payers. However, there is also another possibility, which is that the payer says "no", but additional evidence shows that the drug *is* good value and many patients have lost out from not having access to the treatment during the period the payer refused to list the drug. The company will have lost revenues and the return on an innovation of value to the health care system will have been reduced, with the ensuing reduction in future incentives for innovation.

Payers therefore need to judge the likely costs and benefits of delaying use of a product whilst additional evidence is collected. The costs of collecting that evidence include both the out-of-pocket costs and the loss of patient benefits from use of the product whilst the further evidence is being collected. The benefits are a reduction in uncertainty about the underlying cost-effectiveness of the drug and hence the ability to make a better-informed decision (which is less likely to be wrong). Payers may also seek to reduce uncertainty by pushing for a lower price. At such a price they can be more confident that it will represent a good use of their scarce resources. However, companies may well resist this if they think evidence will support their view of its net benefit to the health care system. In the absence of a compromise, patients will not get access to the medicine until the company provides the additional evidence to support the price it is seeking.

It might appear to be ideal for the manufacturer to have the evidence available at launch to demonstrate cost-effectiveness to the payer. This may not be possible if it relates, for example, to the underlying validity of a surrogate marker for a clinical endpoint or if understanding longer-term effects is key to a judgement on cost-effectiveness. The temptation for the payer in this situation is to say "no" until longer-term evidence is provided. The temptation for the manufacturer is to lobby for approval without having to collect the longer-term evidence. The option of CED (a "yes but") is, in these circumstances, potentially attractive to payers and companies. It enables patients to get access to new drugs with a positive incremental benefit over existing treatments whist additional evidence is being collected.

As well as being a feasible compromise, CED can be seen as likely to produce a socially optimal outcome where the additional evidence is likely to be of value and the current best estimate is that the drug will represent value for money. However, there are some challenges that need to be overcome in order for this to be the case. The most important are:

- It has to be feasible to collect the evidence required whilst the drug is listed by the payer. It may, for example, not be possible to enrol patients into a clinical trial when they can have access to the drug outside of the trial. Evidence can be collected in these circumstances from an observational study or from a trial conducted in another health care system. However, both may raise issues about the quality of the evidence generated: in one case around confounding; in the other around the generalisability of data from one setting to another.

- There is the question of who will bear the risk of the initial assessment of value being wrong. This is in part linked to the question of whether there is an agreement in place. In the absence of an agreement there is a danger of opportunism on both sides. The company may not collect the data in the expectation that the payer will not be able to reverse its adoption decision (patients will protest and/or prescribers will ignore the decision). The payer may refuse to award a higher price or broader use even if the evidence supports the company's claims.

- An agreement to collect data and adjust price will have costs attached to it. In part these will reflect evidence collection costs, although there may be additional costs, for example administrative costs.

There is also likely to be another source of uncertainty for the payer. Even if agreement is reached on the price and use of the drug, the drug still may not be used in the agreed target patient group. We can call this utilisation uncertainty. It can be dealt with via *ex ante* testing of likely response or *ex post* testing of actual response. "Conditional treatment continuation" is a term used by Carlson et al. (2010) to indicate one form of pay-for-performance scheme targeting responders, and, as we noted above, Italian pay-for-performance schemes are targeted on responders. We need to differentiate here, however, between situations in which:

- There is a lot of uncertainty as to who will respond (i.e. achieve some threshold level of improvement) and therefore as to what proportion of the patient population *are* responders. In other words, there remains uncertainty about the cost-effectiveness of the treatment;

- There is a high degree of awareness on the part of the payer of the expected size or proportion of the population for whom the treatment is cost-effective, and who should therefore receive it. The issue here is utilisation uncertainty, i.e making sure these and only these patients receive treatment.

Price-volume agreements are simple, albeit crude, mechanisms to tackle utilisation uncertainty. The numbers of eligible patients can be estimated and the revenues for the company restricted to price times eligible volume. Such an agreement can also allow for lower prices for other subgroups of patients for whom the product is less effective. However, the downside is that there is no guarantee that the product is used on the right patients.

Some new drugs may add substantially to the drug budget and cause payers to worry about exceeding their budget (i.e. affordability) over and above any concerns about value for money (Sendi and Briggs, 2001). In this situation payers may be looking for a revenue cap arrangement.

We summarise the decision choices for the payer in relation to CED and pay-for-performance schemes in Figure 6-1 below.

Numbers and types of schemes

In an earlier review, Carlson et al. (2010) collected evidence on pay-for-performance schemes over the ten year period 1998-2009. Like us, they make a distinction within the category we have termed CED between coverage with the potential for review, for which they found 34 schemes, and pay-for-performance (including conditional treatment continuation schemes) for which they found 24 schemes. Stafinski et al. (2010) found 32 schemes of coverage with the potential for review and 26 examples of pay-for-performance schemes. Both studies pre-date the introduction of the UK PASs in the 2009 PPRS. Towse (2010) found 10 PASs approved by NICE for use in the UK NHS, but these were mostly discount-related. Only one was outcome-related, the bortezomib (Velcade®) responder scheme, which pre-dated the 2009 PPRS and was included in the reviews by both Carlson et al. (2010) and Stafinski et al. (2010). It would therefore appear that in the decade 2000-2009 there were up to 60 CED schemes, of which roughly 55 per cent were CED with the potential for review and 45 per cent were pay-for-performance schemes.

Towse and Garrison (2010) set out examples of the types of schemes we can observe, using the typology set out in Figure 6-1:

- Budget management. Agreements in France, Australia and New Zealand have capped expenditure.

- Achieving effective discounts from list price. The dose-capping agreement that NICE entered into over ranibizumab (Lucentis®) for macular degeneration could be seen as an effective price discount. Cost-effectiveness to NICE was only acceptable if the NHS paid for up to 14 injections per eye of eligible patients. Novartis will bear the costs of treatment beyond this. (NICE Guidance, 2008). NICE recommended ustekinumab (Stelara®) for severe plaque psoriasis on condition that Janssen-Cilag ensures the costs of treating patients weighing more than 100 kilograms will be no more than patients weighing less than 100 kilograms (SCRIP, 2009). This equates roughly to purchasing two vials of ustekinumab (Stelara®) for the price of one.

- Tackling outcomes uncertainty. The UK multiple sclerosis (MS) drugs scheme addresses outcome uncertainty with an observational study of patient health status where price is linked to a cost-per-QALY threshold. In Australia, The agreement for bosentan (Tracleer®) links price to patient survival following an observational study (Wlodarczyk et al. 2006). Money-back guarantees have been offered by a number of companies including Merck US if simvastatin (Zocor®) in combination dietary modifications did not help lower low-density lipoprotein (LDL) and cholesterol levels; Parke-Davis (now Pfizer) in a 2003 UK "outcomes guarantee" for atorvastatin

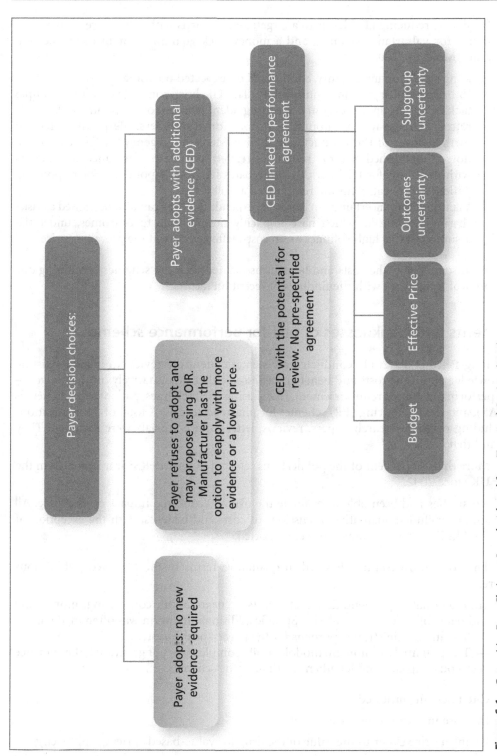

Figure 6-1. Categorising Payer Choices at Launch. Adapted from Towse and Garrison (2010).

(Lipitor®) reducing LDL levels to a target; and Novartis with a "no cure no pay" initiative for valsartan (Diovan®) and a money-back guarantee for nicotine chewing gum (Moldrup, 2005).

- Tackling subgroup uncertainty, conditional on expected outcomes.
  — Via selection or response uncertainty. The UK bortezomib (Velcade®) example tackles subgroup uncertainty, ensuring identification of responders. There is retrospective payer reimbursement for non-responders. Responders receive further doses of the product. The Italian Medicines Agency (AIFA) has, as we noted, established several responder-related pay-for-performance agreements with discounts for trial periods and rebates for non-responders. For responding patients, the treatments are reimbursed at full price.
  — Via utilisation uncertainty. In Australia, expenditure caps can also be viewed as risk-sharing agreements which have implicitly tied revenue to outcomes, under the assumption that high volumes mean cost-ineffective care at the prevailing price.

We discuss below the costs and benefits associated with the schemes combining our theoretical framework with the findings of recent literature.

Benefits and weaknesses of pay-for-performance schemes

Puig-Peiró et al. (2011) conducted a systematic literature review to identify existing knowledge about the costs and benefits – assessed either quantitatively or qualitatively – of performance-based reimbursement, risk sharing (RS) schemes, patient access schemes (PAS), and flexible pricing (FP) schemes for pharmaceuticals. A total of 24 publications including original research papers, reviews, letters and editorials were included. They found that

- More than 40 per cent of the publications referred to the MS RSS implemented in the UK since 2002.

- No studies had been able to evaluate the overall economic impact of a scheme. All studies included qualitative discussions of costs and benefits, with the exception of the MS RSS, where some costs were reported.

The costs most commonly cited in qualitative terms in the reviewed publications were:

- Transactional/implementation costs (costs of negotiation, contracting, monitoring and data collection and analysis). Specific additional mention was often made of:
  — Specific administrative burdens for the payers' health system;
  — The potential for more methodologically complex ways of generating the evidence to push up cost and lengthen the time of the schemes.

Cited benefits included:

- Increase in access to new treatments;

- Paying a price closer to the value of the drug (a "value-based" pricing approach);

- The potential to improve the efficiency of the pharmaceutical market by rewarding innovation; and
- Reducing uncertainty in the payer's decision making process.

In respect of the MS RSS, many challenges were identified. The UK MS RSS was negotiated in 2002 between the UK Department of Health and four pharmaceutical companies supplying MS drugs following NICE's rejection of any use of these drugs by the NHS. It is a 10-year observational study with a historic cohort as a control. It took three years rather than the expected 18 months to recruit 5000 patients at 73 centres. The results of the two-year assessment of accumulated disability of the 5000 patients recruited were not reported until 2009, seven years after the agreement to have a scheme was made. In reporting the results (Boggild et al., 2009), the researchers said that "the outcomes so far obtained in the pre-specified primary analysis suggest a lack of delay in disease progression". However, prices were not adjusted downwards on the grounds that the evidence was not conclusive. This raised issues as to: the design of the study and the time delays in generating the evidence; the enforceability of the contract in relation to the link between prices and outcomes; problems of governance of the scheme including the independence of the Scientific Advisory Group, which was vigorously defended by its chair[iv] (Lilford, 2010); the usefulness of the Expanded Disability Status Scale (EDSS) as the outcome measure; and the impact on the choice of comparator when evaluating subsequent new drugs for the same indications.

Critics also argued that a longer RCT in the UK NHS would have been preferable (McCabe et al., 2010). This seems politically unrealistic, but the same may be said of ignoring the costs associated with evidence collection. The problem is not an unusual one. New therapy in an untreated disease area shows great promise in short-term RCTs using a combination of surrogate markers and some intermediate clinical endpoints. It obtains a license on that basis. The unanswered question is how much long-term health benefit for patients is likely to come from the evidence of short-term improvement in the surrogate endpoint. Waiting for the results of a 10-year post-launch trial is not realistic. It is also likely to be bad economics if pay-for-performance with an effective form of evidence collection and appropriate governance and contract enforceability is a viable option.

Evidence on the costs and effects of other schemes is limited. Although the UK PASs are largely discount arrangements rather than pay-for-performance, the experience is relevant. Williamson (2010) reports on a survey of oncology pharmacists in 31 NHS hospitals. Transaction costs for the NHS were the biggest concern. Variation between the administrative requirements of different schemes added to the problem. There was a concern that in some cases money due back may not have been claimed. In other cases the money came back to the provider hospital but the purchaser (commissioner) was not aware of this. The two schemes "linked to a measurement of clinical response, cetuximab [Erbitux®] and bortezomib [Velcade®], showed a trend towards being the worst. Response-based schemes pose challenges for tracking patients and ensuring claims are

---

[iv] Lilford blamed the design of the study for the failure to draw safe conclusions about effectiveness after two years.

made to refund non-responders". (p111). This is of concern as these are, in effect, pay-for-performance schemes. The Italian pay-for-performance schemes, however, appear to have been well received. This may reflect in part use of a national electronic patient registration system.

The review by Puig-Peiró et al. (2011) thus found a lack of consensus on the welfare consequences of the schemes and their social desirability, partly explained by the scarce evidence available. Some authors recommend outcome-based agreements only in exceptional cases given their complexity and high costs. For example, writing about the MS RSS, Raftery (2010) concludes that "Outcome-based schemes should probably be avoided if at all possible". However, such evidence as we have on the other outcome-based scheme, i.e. the bosentan (Tracleer®) scheme, suggests it worked. Raftery suggests this may be because of use of a smaller patient group (528 patients), a well defined outcome measure (death), and a health system more used to negotiating agreements.

In the literature, identified benefits are countered by significant costs and challenges and therefore the overall balance remains unclear, despite strong opinions regarding one specific scheme (the MS RSS). There is a strong sentiment against outcomes-based schemes. Yet, rewarding products that can be shown to deliver performance (in the form of health gain and other benefits) is likely to be a highly effective way of stimulating innovation.

There appear to be two related problems. The first is a tendency to focus on the negatives of experience to date. Collecting evidence is expensive (in terms both of elapsed time and out-of-pocket cost) and administering a scheme can also be expensive. Yet so far the literature provides little evidence on the overall costs and benefits of schemes undertaken to date. Estimates of the cost of the MS RSS focus on the drug costs at list price. The literature does suggest concern on the part of health care providers of the costs of administering schemes and it is clear that the evidence generated as part of the MS RSS has so far not reduced uncertainty around outcomes and that the contract arrangements have been unsatisfactory. Yet the question is whether use of the schemes could have been expected to produce a better outcome than alternative decision choices on the part of the payer. It is also clear from the literature that there is a great emphasis on CED schemes where outcomes for individual patients are tracked through prospective observational studies of one form or another. This seems to be at the expense of alternatives that may be a more cost-effective use of resources, namely:

• The collection of evidence in another jurisdiction in parallel to the use of the product (Eckerman and Willan, 2009);

• The use of sample studies, rather than including all patients in evidence assessment.

The second problem is that there seems to be a rather naive view about the alternatives to risk-sharing or pay-for-performance arrangements. These are as follows.

• Firstly, more information collected pre-launch, reducing uncertainty, enabling "adopt now" decisions "at-launch". Early payer-company dialogue (in the form of a scientific review) has started regarding evidence requirements for at-launch Health Technology Assessment (HTA). The ability to generate information to reduce uncertainty at launch may be limited, however, by the feasibility of and time delays associated with pre-launch data collection. The assumption seems to be that in this case prices should just be lower, at least until better evidence is generated. Yet prices cannot go up in most markets[v]. Manufacturers are unlikely to be willing to accept permanently lower prices to handle outcome uncertainties at launch.

- Secondly, more delays and sequential resubmission and negotiation with new information and prices. This is unlikely to be efficient, leading to substantial delays in patient access while a cost-effective price is found.

In short, there are no easy options for identifying and rewarding the value of new innovation. Pay-for-performance offers an important way forward to handle uncertainty around the expected value of new innovation in routine clinical practice. It does not require every treated patient to be followed, and performance can be taken from an RCT or other study elsewhere in the world if needed. Costs may come down as payers and manufacturers gain experience of operating these agreements.

REFERENCES

Boggild M, Palace J, Barton P, Ben-Shlomo Y, Bregenzer T, Dobson C, et al. Multiple sclerosis risk sharing scheme: two year results of clinical cohort study with historical comparator. BMJ. 2009; 339: 4677.

Carlson JJ, Sullivan SD, Garrison LP, Neumann PJ, Veenstra DL. Linking payment to health outcomes: a taxonomy and examination of performance-based reimbursement schemes between healthcare payers and manufacturers. Health Policy. 2010;96(3):179-90.

Cook JP, Vernon JA, Manning R. Pharmaceutical risk-sharing agreements. Pharmacoeconomics. 2008;26(7):551-6.

de Pouvourville, G . "Risk-sharing agreements for innovative drugs: a new solution to old problems?" Eur J Health Econ. 2006; 7(3):155-7.

Eckermann S, Willan AR. Expected value of information and decision making in HTA. Health Econ. 2007;16:195-209.

Eckermann S, Willan AR. Globally optimal trial design for local decision making. Health Econ. 2009;18:203-16.

Lilford RJ. Response from chair of scientific advisory committee. BMJ. 2010;341:c3590.

McCabe C, Chilcott J, Claxton K, Tappenden P, Cooper C, Roberts J, et al. Continuing the multiple sclerosis risk sharing scheme is unjustified. BMJ. 2010;340:1786.

Moldrup C. No cure no pay. BMJ. 2005;330(7502):1262-4.

NICE Guidance TA155 Ranibizumab and pegaptanib for treatment of age-related macular degeneration. 2008. Available at: http://guidance.nice.org.uk/TA155/Guidance/pdf/

Pollock A. Pricing Pills by the Results. New York Times; 14th July 2007.

Puig Peiró, R. Mestre-Ferrandiz J, Sussex J, Towse A. Literature review on Patient Access Schemes, Flexible Pricing Schemes and Risk Sharing Agreements for medicines. Podium presentation. ISPOR 14th Annual European Congress, Madrid, Spain: 5-8 November 2011. Available at: http://www.ispor.org/research_pdfs/39/pdffiles/RS1.pdf [Last accessed 28 November 2011]

Raftery J. Multiple sclerosis risk sharing scheme: a costly failure. BMJ. 2010; 40:1672.

Richards RG. MS risk sharing scheme. Some clarification needed. BMJ. 2010;341:3589.

Scolding N. The multiple sclerosis risk sharing scheme. BMJ. 2010;340:2882.

SCRIP. NICE set to recommend Stelara for psoriasis. SCRIP World Pharmaceutical News. August 17th 2009.

Sendi PP, Briggs AH. Affordability and cost-effectiveness: decision-making on the cost-effectiveness plane. Health Econ. 2001;10:675-80.

---

[v] An exception in principle is the UK Flexible Pricing arrangement introduced in the 2009 PPRS. However, this has not been used to date.

Towse A. Value-based pricing, research and development, and patient access schemes. Will the United Kingdom get it right or wrong? Br J Clin Pharmacol. 2010;70(3):360-6.

Towse A, Garrison LP Jr. Can't get no satisfaction? Will pay-for-performance help? Toward an economic framework for understanding performance-based risk-sharing agreements for innovative medical products. Pharmacoeconomics. 2010;28(2):93-102.

Williamson S. Patient access schemes for high-cost cancer medicines. Lancet Oncol. 2010;11(2):111-2.

Wlodarczyk JH, Cleland LG, Keogh AM, McNeil KD, Perl K, Weintraub RG, et al. Public funding of bosentan for the treatment of pulmonary artery hypertension in Australia: cost effectiveness and risk sharing. Pharmacoeconomics. 2006;24(9):903-15.

CHAPTER 7

Drug Price Regulation: Recent Trends and Downstream Neglected Issues

Joan-Ramón Borrell

Introduction

This paper surveys the literature on price regulation in the pharmaceutical sector. After summarizing the well-known results of the available literature, the paper focuses on identifying the remaining open questions, and proposing new research avenues on some neglected issues. It argues that downstream agents such as pharmacists have an important role to play to make price regulation and procurement mechanisms work efficiently, thus stimulating the launch of truly innovative new drugs.

Across most developed countries, cost-based price regulation/procurement schemes have gradually been transformed into two-tiered price controls. On the one hand, many countries have mechanisms of incentive regulation and procurement based on revenue-sharing agreements and demand management for dealing with in-patent drug pricing. On the other hand, most countries have competition-based price regulation/procurement mechanisms that deal with out-of-patent and generic drug pricing.

In both types of schemes, the role of downstream agents such as wholesalers and pharmacists is neglected in most jurisdictions. The evidence in some countries shows how important it is to align the incentives of those agents in order to have welfare-enhancing price regulation and procurement schemes that encourage the introduction of truly innovative drugs that command higher prices, while promoting competition in the out-of-patent segment of the market. Future research is badly needed to gain further insight into how incentives at the downstream end of the industry contribute to securing efficiency in drug pricing.

The paper is organized as follows: Section 2 provides a brief review of the previous literature that shows how countervailing forces play in drug pricing, and the different price regulations and procurement traditions that deal with such forces in the drug industry. Section 3 describes the well known results obtained by this literature, and it suggests that one important question remains open. Section 4 describes how the incentives of downstream agents have been neglected, and how important those incentives are for efficient drug pricing. Section 5 offers some concluding remarks.

Countervailing forces in drug pricing

Pharmaceutical markets are unique in one particular aspect that has not received sufficient attention. Drug pricing is subject to countervailing forces that lead to corner solutions, namely overpricing or underpricing. It is very common to characterize some countries as markets that support excessively high prices (particularly the US, Germany, and others), while others are characterized as markets with excessively low prices (less developed countries and even southern EU countries).

There are some economic fundamentals in drug markets that support both extremes, overpricing and underpricing.

Remark 1. *Overpricing. Insurance creates inelastic demand – patients are less price-sensitive when the insurer is paying the bill (Regan 2007). Demand is also inelastic because access to most medicines requires a prescription from a doctor and pharmacists to dispense the drug. Moreover, doctors and pharmacists are imperfect agents for their patients. They do not fully internalize the impact of their prescription and dispensing decisions on their patients after-treatment net utility function. All these drug-demand particularities drive prices up. Additionally, patents restrict competition and allow innovators to price medicines above marginal cost and obtain quasi-rents that should boost revenues enough to recoup R&D sunk costs. This also encourages price spikes.*

Remark 2. *Underpricing. At the same time, direct government intervention via regulation or public provision of drugs, indirect government intervention in health and pharmaceutical insurance, or even a concentrated private insurance market, leads to buyer power. Such countervailing power may drive the market to the other corner solution. The industry is prone to suffer the classical hold-up problem. As R&D is a cost already sunk at the drug-launch stage, government or insurers are tempted to expropriate the industry by setting prices close to marginal cost, well under average costs that internalize R&D outlays, for instance by circumventing patent rights and avoiding payment of the fair share of global R&D costs according to the country income.*

Both corner solutions have short-run and long-run undesired consequences:

- Overpricing is undesired because it induces excessively high R&D and re-directs marginal research efforts toward drugs for which demand imperfections are more acute. Additionally, overpricing leads to overprovision by physicians and pharmacists when they are imperfect agents for their patients (Duggan and Scott Morton 2008, and Evans 1974)[i].

- Underpricing is undesired because it induces excessively low R&D and drives marginal research effort towards drugs less prone to suffer from the hold-up problem, such as drugs that treat the conditions of patients located in countries with a stronger commitment to contributing to pay their fair share of R&D costs. Additionally,

---

[i] E.g. the case of pharmacists if they are remunerated with a fixed percentage margin on final prices.

underpricing leads to underprovision by physicians and pharmacists when they are imperfect agents for their patients[ii].

Across countries, there are two distinct regulatory/procurement traditions in drug price control.

One is focused on across-the-board price regulations. Usually, countries with under-developed public or private health insurance schemes are prone to using government plain regulation (command and control) to make sure that private parties do have access to essential pharmaceutical treatments.

Such price regulation is usually non-sophisticated – it applies extensive product-by-product cost-based ex-manufacturing pricing and it restricts or forbids price increases. In this tradition, wholesalers and pharmacists are usually reimbursed using a cost-based plus fixed-margin formula.

By contrast, there is another tradition more focused on government procurement schemes. It has usually been the intervention tradition in the countries that already have a public and/or private health insurance market.

This second tradition uses agreements between the health insurer and the provider of drugs that roughly take the form of rate-of-return or revenue-sharing price regulations.

Many of the countries in this tradition have additionally developed incentive-based pricing mechanisms to cope with the imperfect agent problem – they usually include some form of remuneration fees and reimbursement mechanisms to encourage doctors and pharmacists to provide their services more efficiently. They also use formulary pricing, de-listings and cost-effectiveness analysis to manage the drug demand that they are covering. When physicians and pharmacists become better agents for their patients, overpricing leads to underprovison of drugs. By contrast, underpricing leads to overprovision of drugs.

As a result of the accumulation of regulation/procurement strategies, what we actually see is a mix of three types of schemes:

- Cost-based price regulations: regulatory mechanisms used by governments or insurers focused on auditing drug firms', wholesalers' and retailers' costs. They have also gradually introduced mechanisms to compare the price of drugs across countries (cross-country external price referencing).

- Incentive-based price regulations: price regulations and procurement mechanisms focused on containing escalating drug costs of in-patent drugs with very few substitutes by reaching agreements with providers (revenue sharing), and by directing agents' incentives to contain costs and manage demand.

- Competiton-based price regulations: price regulations and procurement mechanisms such as reference pricing and clawback clauses that drive prices down by the competitive interplay of different providers of out-of-patent branded and generic drugs.

[ii] It might not be so undesired if underpricing discouraged wasteful research expenditure on me-too products, while focusing the industry on developing "drastic innovations" as suggested by Ganuza and Llobet (2008). Governments and insurers are less likely to underprice drugs that turn out to be therapeutic breakthroughs.

Sood et al. (2009) offer evidence on the trends in the use of all these mechanisms between 1992 and 2004 in 19 OECD countries. Table 7-1 shows that the overall picture displays a constant increase in the use of price regulation and procurement schemes to control drug prices.

Direct price controls negotiated between government and public health insurers is used by 16 countries, up from 13 in 1992. Apart from such direct controls, all countries are increasingly using incentive-based regulations and competition-based reimbursement mechanisms:

- Incentive-based regulations:
  — The last two decades have witnessed an upsurge of cost-effectiveness evaluations (from only 2 countries in 1992 to 10 countries in 2004) used during price negotiations between insurers and drug firms when launching a new in-patent drug.
  — Given the spike of introductory prices of breakthrough innovative drugs, many countries have also introduced degressive pharmacy fees, although most are fixed fees that do not allow pharmacies to offer discounts to patients or insurers (from 5 countries in 1992 to 10 in 2004).
  — Another mechanism that has been introduced by many countries is global budget controls that cap the increase in the expenditures funded by insurers at company or drug level (only 1 country had global budget controls in 1992, while 6 had them in 2004).
  — Other countries, such as the UK, have continued to use profit controls. By 2004, a further two countries had joined the UK in using this type of control mechanism.
  — Finally, two countries had introduced prescribing budgets at physician- or health-center level by 2004.

- Competition-based regulations: in parallel to incentive-based regulations for in-patent drugs, there has been a trend of introducing regulations to spur competition in the out-of-patent segment of the market.
  — Up to 13 countries mandated substituting any brand-name drug with its cheaper generic version in 2004, while only 3 countries were mandating substitution in 1992.
  — Additionally, up to 7 countries had generic reference pricing schemes in 2004, while only 2 had such reference pricing in 1992.
  — Up to 6 countries had extended reference pricing to not only brand-generics groups, but also to therapeutic classes of drugs combining more than one active ingredient in 2004.
  — There were only 3 countries with such therapeutic reference pricing regulations in 1992.
  — Finally, up to 5 countries had incentives in place to encourage doctors to prescribe generics in 2004, while only 2 countries had such incentives in 1992.

The literature studying the market for pharmaceuticals has intensively analyzed many of the different regulatory and procurement mechanisms outlined above. Theory and empirical evidence has analyzed the effects of most of these schemes. We will now turn to survey the well-known results of the available literature, which aspects remain as open questions, and finally which are neglected issues that merit further research.

Table 7-1. Trends in drug price controls in the OCDE 1992-2004

	1992	2004
Direct price control	13	16
Incentive-based regulations		
Cost-effectiveness evaluations	2	10
Degressive pharmacy fee	5	10
Global budget controls	1	6
Profit controls	1	3
Prescribing budgets	0	2
Competition-based regulations		
Generic substitution	3	24
Generic reference pricing	2	7
Therapeutic reference pricing	3	6
Generic prescribing incentives	2	5

Source: Sood N. et al (2009)

Well-known results

We will start by reviewing the well-know results from the literature on drug pricing. We will then move on to review the literature on the impact of cost-base regulations, the impact of incentive regulations on pricing, and finally the effect of competition-based regulations.

Drug pricing

Cross-country studies of drug pricing had traditionally shown that prices in less interventionist countries such as the US or Germany had higher ex-factory drug prices. However, thess results have been clearly contested in the more recent literature that has been able to estimate pricing differences in a more consistent and robust manner.

Danzon and Chao (2000b) and Cabrales and Jiménez-Martín (2007) show that after controlling for drug characteristics and income, the US does not have higher prices than other developed countries. Borrell (2007) shows how drug pricing for HIV-AIDS drugs in developing countries depends mostly on income, patent protection and time since launch in the US, and that large pharmaceutical firms price-discriminate across countries and time.

The most recent evidence is offered by Sood et al. (2009). This paper shows that price regulations have a direct and strong impact on drug firm revenues, but not so on drug pricing.

Controls have three different effects on expenditures.

- First, they may eventually be constraining insured demand, and in so doing they may be countervailing the force that drives overpricing if demand is insured. Regan (2007) offered clear evidence that the price of branded medicines in the US increases as the fraction of insured patients increases. Each additional 10% fraction of insured patients drives prices up by 5.1% in the case of 18 oral solid branded drugs that experienced initial generic entry between 1998 and 2002.

- Second, regulations may be managing demand towards older and more cost-effective drugs, and generics. Regan (2007) also finds a strong reduction in the revenues of branded drugs from insured patients when generics become available, much stronger than the reduction in revenues from non-insured or Medicaid patients.

- Finally, price regulations are having an indirect impact on the product choice set probably having more relevant impact on welfare.
    — Firstly, although never estimated, there is widespread concern that price regulation may reduce revenues and profits from innovation. So a first-order concern is that price regulation may, as suggested by Sood et al. (2009), improve the welfare of current generations but hurt future generations by reducing the pace of innovation. Acemoglu and Linn (2004) offer evidence that in the pharmaceutical industry the introduction of new chemical entities respond to anticipated changes in market size with a lead of 10-20 years. The relationship between of the introduction of drugs and regulation has only been identified and quantified robustly in the case of generics. Moreno, Puig and Borrell (2009) show how the introduction of generic reference pricing and mandatory substitution rules had strong and persistent negative impacts on the introduction of generics in Spain.
    — Secondly, it has been clearly identified that price regulations lead to drug launch delays (Danzon et al., 2005 and Kyle, 2007). Firms may prefer to delay the launch in a low-price country because the low price may spill over other countries when launch prices are negotiated or when prices are subject to external cross-country referencing. Additionally, firms may delay the launch of new drugs in the country that is the source for parallel trading activities.
    — Finally, it is also well reported and identified that firms get around price regulations by using presentation proliferation or brand proliferation, through licensing and launching "me-too" products (Ellison and Ellison, 2007). The presentation, brand names or me-too chemical entities allow firms to diversify in price negotiations with the regulators, and to hinder competition from generics, as well as cross-country price comparisons and parallel traders.

Literature on price controls

To understand how drug price controls have had an impact on such pricing results.

With respect to cost-based price regulations, it is well known that auditing is imperfect and that any regulation mechanism ends in some sort of price negotiation between insurers and firms, or some sort of external referencing mechanism.

As we have seen before, Sood et al. (2009) show that direct price regulations (including external referencing schemes) were used in 16 out of 19 developed countries in 2004.

Cost-based regulations lead to the overprovision of varieties. See Borrell, Costas, Nonell (2005) comparing the number of presentations and brands in Spain versus the UK.

Cost-based regulations drive also launch delays, parallel trading, and the proliferation of local licensing as a mechanism to obtain favorable outcomes from price negotiations when insurers and governments use industrial criteria when setting launch prices. See Borrell (2007) on the case of HIV-AIDS drugs in developing countries.

Profit controls do not "bite" expenditures (see Sood et al., 2009). These controls usually take the form of a cost- plus rate-of-return regulation, and then have the well known impact of such regulations. See Borrell (1999) regarding the effect of the UK Pharmaceutical Price Regulation Scheme, and Duggan & Scott Morton (2006) for the case of Medicaid. Profit controls encourage firm diversification and investments that can be passed through. Profit controls are then additional instruments of industrial policy rather than effective mechanisms of expenditure control.

With respect to incentive-based regulations, Sood et al. (2009) show that incentive-based mechanisms such as global and physician budgets do "bite" expenditures. However, they also show that there is what may be called a law of decreasing returns from using more and more regulations to curb expenditure.

There is a large amount of literature that analyzes the dynamics of competition among out-of-patent and generic drugs.

There is substantial evidence that formularies and managed demand for pricing of non-unique drugs have a strong impact on curbing prices and expenditures (Elzinga & Mills, 1997, Borrell, 2003, Duggan & Scott Morton, 2008).

Table 7-2 shows that the introduction of generics and reference pricing in Spain in 2003 changed the dynamics of the health system public pharmaceutical expenditure. From an average annual growth rate of 9% before reference pricing, the drug bill grew by 6% after its introduction. The driver of this shift in dynamics is the change in the average annual growth rate in the price per prescription: from being the largest driver of expenditure by growing at a rate of 5% before the introduction of reference pricing, it slowed down to a growth rate of 1%.

Figure 7-1 shows in a simple but illustrative way the approximate savings in the Spanish Health System drug bill after the setup of a reference pricing system that curbed the prices of drugs with generic equivalents. Savings were in the region of 18% of the drug bill in 2009 (EUR 2,571m).

The literature clearly shows that the impact of generics on prices depends strongly on the substitution and reimbursement rules. The entry of generics drives average prices down, but it can foster higher prices for branded products (the well known generics paradox, the last evidence of which can be found in Regan 2007). Mandatory substitution is a key factor for decreasing the prices of brand products with generic equivalents. And, as we will discuss below, downstream reimbursement rules are the leading decisive factor for generic pricing competition.

Table 7-2. Growth Spanish Health System Drug Bill

Period	Drug Bill	Price per prescription	Number of prescription	Population	Prescription per person
1996–2003	9%	5%	4%	1%	3%
2003–2009	6%	1%	5%	2%	3%

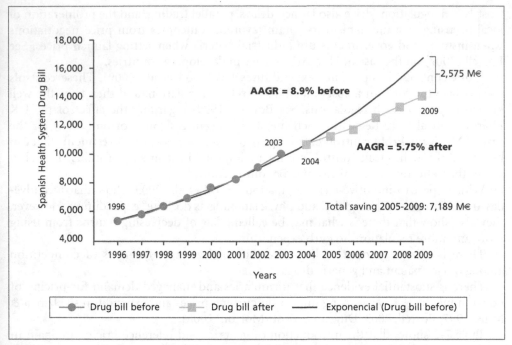

Figure 7-1. Spanish National Health System Drug Bill Before and After Reference Pricing

Furthermore, generic reference pricing not only drives prices down, it also slows down generic entry (Moreno, Puig and Borrell, 2009). This may lead to lower prices with a smaller number of generics, or it can deter entry and the trend towards lower prices.

Open question: parallel trading

There is an important issue that is still open to discussion among economists and lawyers, particularly in the EU, regarding price controls – the question of the welfare effects of parallel trading.

Valletti and Szymanski (2005) and Valletti (2006) have shown that parallel trade prevents firms from optimally setting different prices in different markets, and then profits are not maximized and incentives to innovate are reduced. However, this welfare detrimental effect of parallel trading depends on the assumption that firms are the ones that freely decide on pricing and investments in innovation. By contrast, Rey (2003), Grossman and Lai (2006) and Sauri (2007) obtain different results when such assumption does not hold.

In particular, Sauri (2007) shows that if prices are set in a bargaining exchange with governments, parallel trading may have beneficial welfare effects. In particular, parallel trade does not allow governments in low-income countries to free-ride on other governments' higher willingness to pay for innovation. Parallel trade is welfare-enhancing because it makes governments responsible for the uniform price that will prevail in all markets. According to Sauri (2007), parallel trade has this wefare-enhancing property only if the differences in willingness to pay for innovation across countries is small.

This is therefore an open question which is especially relevant in the EU. Parallel trading of drugs has been upheld by the European Court of Justice's ruling in Merk v. Primecrown[iii]. However, the European Court of First Instance has recently limited parallel trading to those cases where it does not have detrimental effects on the incentives to innovate[iv].

Neglected issue: downstream incentives and competition

The role of downstream regulation and competition in containing expenditure and increasing welfare in the pharmaceutical sector is a neglected issue in the literature. As far as I am aware, only Danzon and Chao (2000a) have studied the extent to which not only price regulation, but also the regulation of pharmacy margins and discounts, undermine price competition. However, they are not able to clearly identify the effect of ex-factory price regulation and downstream margin regulation on price competition among generics and brand-name drugs[v]. Danzon and Furukawa (2011) for their part, simply highlight this is as an important issue when studying competition among generics in the market. But again, they neither model nor identify how downstream incentives drive generic drug pricing.

Table 7-3 shows the main regulations affecting the pharmacy sector in Europe. In many European countries it is common for entry regulations restricting the number of pharmacies in a given geographic area to be particularly stringent. ÖBIG's (2006) report for the European Commission and COFV & FEFE (2007) show that 20 out of 27 EU Member States operate entry restrictions[vi], a situation that contrasts markedly with that in the US and Canada, where no restrictions are operative. In 6 out of these 20 EU Member States with entry restrictions, there are explicit distance regulations that require pharmacies to locate far away from each other (from 150 to 400 minimum distance regulations). This is the case of Austria, Greece, Hungary, Portugal, Slovenia and Spain. In only 3 out of these 20 EU Member States there is free entry of pharmacies selling OTC drugs and drugs to patients that pay out of their pocket. However, state-controlled health insurer organizations or public services limit the number of contracting pharmacies – this is the case of the United Kingdom, Ireland and the Netherlands. COFV & FEFE (2007) report that in 16 out of 25 EU Member States only licensed pharmacists can own and open a pharmacy to dispense drugs to the public. In the US, there is usually freedom of establishment

---

[iii] Case C-267-268/95. Merck & Co. Inc. v. Primecrown Limited. Court of Justice of the European Communities. Press Release No 58/96, 5 December 1996.

[iv] Case T-168/01. GlaxoSmithKline v. EC Commission. Court of First Instance of the European Communities. Press Release No 79/06, 27 September 2006.

[v] Danzon and Chao (2000a) estimates suggest that pharmacy regulations, particularly relating to pack size and bulk dispensing and margins, hamper the incentives of drug firms to offer volume discounts to pharmacists.

[vi] In most Member States the establishment of new pharmacies is restricted on geographic and demographic criteria. Only in the UK and the Netherlands entry is restricted by the contracts with the tax-funded health care organizations. Mossialos and Mrazek (2003) also report that entry is restricted in Norway.

by any person or corporation with the single requirement to hire licensed professional pharmacists to serve the public. Paradoxically, there are some states in the US that forbid pharmacists from owning or running pharmacies (Abood, 2007). COFV & FEFE (2007) also report that in 10 out of 27 EU Member States there are state-owned pharmacies open to the public, usually to cover dispensing needs in small villages, but also as a public monopoly in the case of Sweden.

Furthermore, European entry restrictions are typically coupled with price or retail margin regulations. ÖBIG (2006) reported to the European Commission that 18 out of 25 Member States set pharmacy markups by regulation and discounts are not allowed, while the remaining 7 set maximum markups or fees for services while allowing free discounts to customers.

While regulations that restrict the entry of new firms into a market by fixing the number of firms that can supply that particular market are common in industries such as finance (e.g. banking and insurance), transport (e.g. taxis and buses), retailing (e.g. supermarkets, alcohol and tobacco) and the professions (e.g. pharmacists and solicitors), in Europe there is an ongoing discussion as to whether these entry restrictions serve public interests or whether they benefit private incumbents. At the same time, a growing body of literature has begun to assess the impact of these restrictions and their appropriateness with regard to the aims they pursue.

Schaumans and Verboven (2008) and Borrell and Fernández-Villadangos (2009) assess the impact of pharmacy entry regulations on the number of pharmacies competing downstream, and also the excess margins and rents that such restrictions offer to pharmacy owners in the case of Belgium and Spain respectively in non-metropolitan municipalities. The number of competitors downstream is reduced by as much as 50% in Belgium due to entry regulation in municipalities.

The data on ex-factory per capita pharmaceutical spending compiled by OECD and cross-country information on margins allow us to compare the share of upstream and downstream expenditure across developed countries. Figure 7-2 shows that per capita spending in US$ at PPP at the upstream and downstream segments of the industry is highly correlated.

Table 7-3. Downstream regulations across countries in Europe

	Number	out of	
Ownership restricted	16	27	59%
Pharmacist-owned only	15	27	56%
State-owned only	1	27	4%
State-owned pharmacies	9	27	33%
Entry restricted	20	27	74%
Distances regulated	6	27	22%
NHS contracts restricted	3	27	11%
Margins regulated	25	25	100%
Fixed or degressive margins	18	25	72%
Maximum margins	7	25	28%

Figures 7-2 and 7-3 show this correlation. The question that remains to be studied is whether the countries that manage to introduce competition downstream ultimately achieve lower-than-average ex-factory per capita spending.

In Spain, Borrell and Merino (2007) show that the regulation of pharmacy margins and the formal prohibition of rebates is neglecting the increase in competition among generic manufacturers. Those manufacturers are offering pharmacies volume discounts that are not passed on to payers.

For a group of 16 active ingredients for which there is a number of generic firms competing in the market, volume discounts ranged from 17% to 38% (with an average of 34%). The setup of the generic reference pricing system in Spain allows pharmacists to choose which generic is dispensed when all are priced at the lowest price. This mechanism encourages efficient generic firms to offer discounts to pharmacists rather than offering a lower ex-factory price to the payer.

Figure 7-4 shows using the simple set-up suggested by Motta (2004) that an efficient incumbent with marginal costs equal to c_I will offer a preemptive discount to a pharmacist equal to the grey area in the figure, to prevent the entry of any other less efficient generic firm with marginal cost equal c_E to given a reference price equal to P_R, where $P_R > c_E > c_I$. The discount will be precisely equal to the difference between the reference price and the less efficient firm's marginal cost plus some epsilon, e: $P_R - c_E + e$.

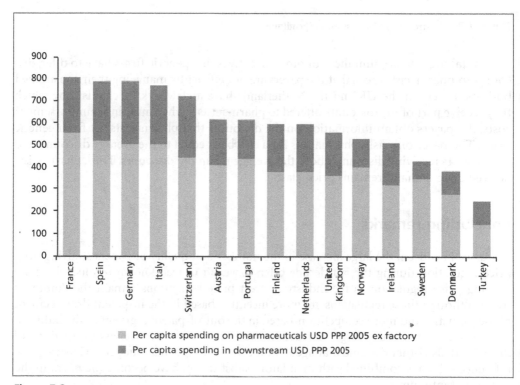

Figure 7-2. Downstream vs. Upstream Spending

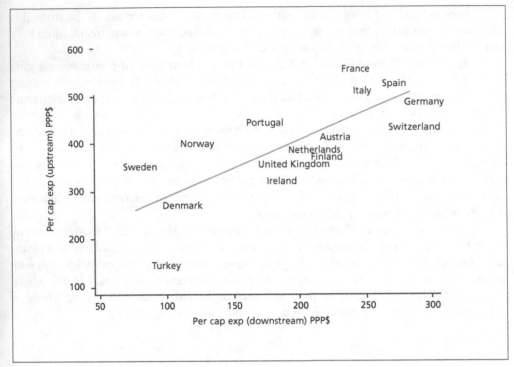

Figure 7-3. Upstream and Downstream expenditure

Not taking into account the economic incentives that generic firms have to offer, discounts to pharmacists mean that the payers are not efficiently managing their constrained budgets. Payers in the UK and the Netherlands have a clawback mechanism by which they receive part of the discounts offered to pharmacists – when auditing reimbursement costs, the payers obtain information on the discounts that pharmacists get from generic firms. The payer only asks pharmacists for a clawback equal to the average discount, and pharmacists receiving discounts above the average retain the discounts. Thus, pharmacist-derived drug demand remains price-elastic.

Concluding remarks

As we have seen, the large increase in the number and quality of papers studying drug price regulation during the last decade offers a wealth of well-known results, which are shaping price regulation in the industry. Direct price regulations remain the dominant trend, although those regulations are more incentive-based in the in-patent drug segment of the industry, and more competition-based in the out-of-patent segment of the industry.

We have witnessed a large increase in the use of cost-effectiveness evaluations of drugs, and also other demand management mechanisms (such as budgets). Generic price reference schemes combined with mandatory substitution have become the norm in the out-of-patent segment.

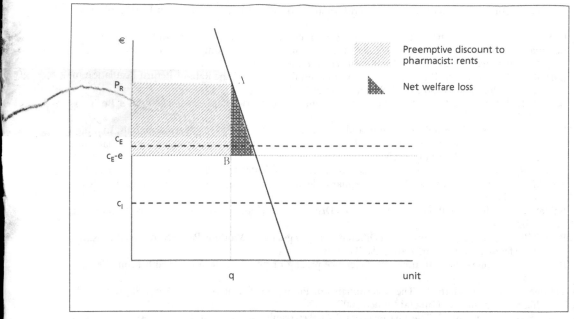

Figure 7-4. Analysing discounts

By contrast, there are some open questions that merit some further research. In particular, the welfare implications of parallel trading within developed countries remains a contentious issue. And cost-effectiveness evaluations are just starting to grow. Both are important to make drug controls work in favor of encouraging more innovative product launches in the in-patent segment while imposing tougher competition in the out-of-patent segment.

Furthermore, the recent literature has neglected the downstream activities of this industry. Regulation downstream is particularly damaging any prospects of utilizing competition-based mechanisms to govern pricing in the out-of-patent segment of the industry. Downstream regulations need to be evaluated by means of the test that the European Court of Justice is using to guarantee the fundamental freedoms of circulation and establishment – regulations should be necessary, adequate, proportional and non-discriminatory to serve the objective of public service they aim to achieve. Much research is to be conducted to expand our knowledge on this issue.

REFERENCES

Abood R. Pharmacy Practice and the Law. 5th ed. Sudbury (MA): Jones and Bartlett Publishers; 2007.

Aronsson T, Bergman M, Rudholm N. The impact of generic drug competition on brand name market shares. Evidence from micro data. Review of Industrial Organization. 2001;19:425-35.

Arruñada B. Managing Competition in Professional Services and the Burden of Inertia. In: Ehlermann C-D, Atanasiu I, editors. European Competition Law Annual 2004: The Relationship between

Competition Law and the (Liberal) Professions. Oxford and Portland, Oregon: Hart Publishing; 2006. p. 51-71.

Bae JP. Drug patent expirations and the speed of generic entry. Health Services Research. 1997;32:187-201.

Bergman M, Rudholm N. The relative importance of actual and potential competition: Empirical evidence from the pharmaceuticals market. J Industrial Economics. 2003;51:455-67.

Borrell JR. Pharmaceutical Price Regulation: A Study on the Impact of the Rate-of-Return Regulation in the UK. Pharmacoeconomics. 1999;15(3):291-303.

Borrell JR. Drug price differentials caused by formularies and price caps. Int J Economics Business. 2003;10:37-50.

Borrell JR, Costas A, Nonell R. Regulation and competition in the market for pharmaceuticals. In: Puig-Junoy J, editor. The public financing of pharmaceuticals: An economic approach. Cheltenham and Northampton: Edward Elgar; 2005. p. 59-83.

Borrell JR, Merino A. Los beneficios de una competencia incipiente: descuentos y bonificaciones a oficinas de farmacia. In: Cases L, editor. Anuario de la Competencia 2006. Madrid: Fundación ICO-Marcial Pons; 2007.

Borrell JR. Pricing and Patents of HIV/AIDS Drugs in Developing Countries. Applied Economics. 2007;39(4):505-18.

Borrell JR. Assessing Excess Profits from Different Entry Regulations. Working Paper Num. 2009-03. Xarxa de Referencia en Economia Aplicada, Barcelona.

Brekke KR, Königbauer I, Straume OR. Reference pricing of pharmaceuticals. J Health Econ. 2007;26: 613-42.

Cabrales A, Jiménez-Martín S. The Determinants of Pricing in Pharmaceuticals: Are U.S. prices really higher than those of Canada? Mimeo 2007.

Costa-Font J, Puig-Junoy J. The pharmaceutical market regulation in Spain: Is drug cost-containment under question? J Pharmaceuticals Finance, Economics and Policy. 2005;13:33-49.

COFV & FEFE. Marco Legal Comparado de la Farmacia en Europa. Colegio Oficial de Farmacéuticos de Valencia y Federación Empresarial de Farmacéuticos Españoles; 2007.

Danzon PM, Chao WL. Does regulation drive out competition in pharmaceutical markets? J Law Econ. 2000;43:311-57.

Danzon PM, Chao WL. Cross-national price differences for pharmaceuticals: how large, and why? J Health Econ. 2000;19:159-95.

Danzon PM, Ketcham JD. Reference pricing of pharmaceuticals for Medicare: Evidence from Germany, the Netherlands and New Zealand. Forum for Health Economics & Policy, 7. 2004 (Frontiers in Health Policy Research), Article 2. Retrieved from http://www.bepress.com/fhep/7/2.

Danzon PM, Wang YR, Wang L. The impact of price regulation on the launch delay of new drugs – evidence from twenty-five major markets in the 1990s. Health Economics. 2005;14:269-92.

Danzon PM, Furukawa M. Cross-National Evidence on Generic Pharmaceuticals: Pharmacy vs. Physician-Driven Markets. NBER Working Paper Series; 2011.

Daunfeldt SO, Rudholm N, Bergström F. Entry into Swedish retail and wholesale trade markets. Rev Industrial Organization. 2006;29:213-25.

Daunfeldt SO, Rudholm N. Revenues as a proxy for profits: A cautionary note. Applied Economic Letters. 2009;16:679-81.

de Pouvourville, G (2006). "Risk-sharing agreements for innovative drugs: a new solution to old problems?" Eur J Health Econ. 7(3):155-7.

Domínguez B, Ganuza JJ, Llobet G. R&D in the Pharmaceutical Industry: A World of Small Innovations. Manage Sci. 2008.55:539-551.

Duggan M, Morton SF. The Effect of Medicare Part D on Pharmaceutical Prices and Utilization. Mimeo; 2008.

Duggan M, Morton SF. "The Distortionary Effects of Government Procurement: Evidence for Medicaid Prescription Drug Purchasing. Quarterly Journal of Economics. 2006;1:30.

Ekelund M. Generic entry before and after the introduction of reference prices. In: Ekelund M, editor. Competition and innovation in the Swedish pharmaceutical market. Dissertation. Chapter 4. Stockholm School of Economics; 2001. p. 1-17.

Ekelund M, Persson B. Pharmaceutical pricing in a regulated market. Review of Economics and Statistics. 2003;85:298-306.

Ellison G, Ellison SF. Strategic Entry Deterrece and the Behaviour of Pharmaceutical Incumbents Prior to Patent Expiration. NBER Working Paper; 2007.

European Commission. Pharmaceutical Sector Inquiry. Preliminary Report. DG Competition Staff Working Paper, Brussels; 2008.

Evans R. Supplier-Induced Demand: Some Empirical Evidence and Implications. In: Perlman M, editor. The Economics of Health and Medical Care. London: Macmillan; 1974. p. 162-73.

Frank RG, Salkever DS. Generic entry and the pricing of pharmaceuticals. J Economics Management Strategy. 1997;6:75-90.

Grabowski HG, Vernon JM. Brand loyalty, entry, and price competition in pharmaceuticals after the 1984 drug act. J Law Econ. 1992;35:331-50.

Grossman G, Lai E. International Protection of Intellectual Property. Am Econ Rev. 2004;94:1635-53.

Hollis A. How do brands 'own generics' affect pharmaceutical prices? Rev Industrial Organization. 2005;27:329-50.

Hong SH, Shepherd MD, Scoones D, Wan TTH. Product-line extensions and pricing strategies of brand-name drugs facing patent expiration. J Managed Care Pharmacy. 2005;11:746-54.

Hudson J. Generic take-up in the pharmaceutical market following patent expiry: A multi-country study. Int Rev Law Econ. 2000;24:103-12.

Iizuka T. Generic entry in a regulated pharmaceutical market. Japanese Econ Rev. 2009;60:63-81.

Jansson E. Libre competencia frente a regulación en la distribución minorista de medicamentos. Rev Econ Apl. 1999;19:85-112.

Königbauer I. Advertising and generic market entry. J Health Econ. 2006;26:286-305.

Kyle M. Pharmaceutical Price Controls and Entry Strategies. Rev Econ Statistics. 2007;89(1):88-99.

López-Casasnovas G, Puig-Junoy J. Review of the literature on reference pricing. Health Policy. 2000;54:87-123.

Magazzini L, Pammolli F, Riccaboni M. Dynamic competition in pharmaceuticals: Patent expiry, generic penetration, and industry Structure. Eur J Health Econ. 2004;5:175-82.

Mestre-Ferrándiz J. The impact of generic goods in the pharmaceutical industry. Health Economics. 1999;8:599-612.

Moreno I, Puig J, Borrell JR. Generic Entry into the Regulated Spanish Pharmaceutical Market. Rev Industrial Organization. 2009;34(4):373-88.

Mossialos E, Mrazek M. The Regulation of Pharmacies in Six Countries. Report prepared for the Office of Fair Trading London; 2003.

Motta M. Competition Policy. Theory and Practice. Cambridge University Press; 2004.

Nuscheller R. Physician reimbursement, time, consistency, and the quality of care. J Institutional Theoretical Econ. 2003;159:302-22.

ÖBIG. Surveying, Assessing and Analyzing the Pharmaceutical Sector in the 25 EU Member States. Report Commissioned by the DG Competition - European Commission. Brussels: Office for Official Publications of the European Communities; 2006.

Puig-Junoy J. Incentives and pharmaceutical reimbursement reforms in Spain. Health Policy. 2004;67:149-65.

Puig-Junoy J. Los medicamentos genéricos pagan el precio de ser referencia. Rev Admin Sanit. 2004;2: 35-59.

Puig-Junoy J. The impact of generic reference pricing interventions in the statin market. Health Policy. 2007;84:14-29.

Regan TL. Generic entry, price competition, and market segmentation in the prescription drug market. Int J Industrial Organization. 2007.

Reiffen D, Ward ME. Generic drug industry dynamics. Review of Economics and Statistics. 2005;87:37-49.

Reiffen D, Ward ME. Branded generics' as a strategy to limit cannibalization of pharmaceutical markets. Managerial and Decision Economics. 2007;28:251-65.

Rey P. The impact of parallel imports on prescription medicines. Mimeo. 2003.

Rudholm N. Entry and the number of firms in the Swedish pharmaceuticals market. Rev Industrial Organization. 2001;19:351-64.

Rudholm N. Competition and substitutability in the Swedish pharmaceuticals market. Applied Econ. 2003;35:1609-17.

Saha A, Grabowski H, Birnbaum H, Greenberg P. Generic competition in the US pharmaceutical industry. Int J Econ Business. 2006;13:15-38.

Sauri L. Price Bargaining, Parallel Trade and Incentives to Innovate. European University Institute, Mimeo; 2007.

Scott Morton F. Entry decisions in the generic pharmaceutical industry. RAND J Econ. 1999;30:421-40.

Scott Morton F. Barriers to entry, brand advertising, and generic entry in the U.S. pharmaceutical industry. Int J Industrial Organization. 2000;18:1085-104.

Segura P. The peculiar patent and generic situation in Spain. Scrip Magazine. 1997;58:23-5.

Schaumans C, Verboven F. Entry and regulation. Evidence from health care professions. RAND J Econ. 2008;22:490-504.

Szymanski S, Valletti TM. Parallel trade, price discrimination, investment and price caps. Economic Policy. 2005;20:705-49.

Valletti TM. Differential pricing, parallel trade, and the incentive to invest. J Int Econ. 2006;70(1):314-24.

Waterson M. Retail Pharmacy in Melbourne: Actual and Optimal Densities. J Industrial Economics. 1993;41:403-19.